Learning to be a Widow

LEARNING TO BE A WIDOW

STORIES OF LOVE, LOSS AND LESSONS LEARNED ALONG THE WAY

BY
GWEN ROMAGNOLI

Cover design by Giancarlo Romagnoli
Author photo by Franco Romagnoli

Print ISBN: 978-0-7867-5645-2
ebook ISBN: 978-0-7867-5646-9

Distributed by
Argo Navis Author Services
www.argonavisdigital.com

For Franco

Table of Contents

Preface, ix

Introduction, xii

CHAPTERS

Learning to Be a Widow   3

Extraordinary Measures   6

Finding Franco's Manuscript   12

The First Week   15

Devil in a Blue Dress   19

Those Wretched TV Ads   23

Bicycling   28

An Empty Space   32

Traveling with Lasix   35

Franco's Father   41

Meeting Dr. Goggins   44

Going on Dialysis   49

Indianapolis   53

Becoming Midwesterners   68

The Ring   75

Be Perky   78

Advice Givers   81

What's Left Behind   84

Admit One   87

The Widow Sign   90

Single Serving   93

The Number Twelve—An Anniversary   96

A Change of Season   99

Tinkering   102

The Wedding   107

Hearing His Voice   112

Filippello Park   115

Cemeteries   118

A Full-Time Job   121

In the System   126

All the Things People Give Me to Read   129

Totaled   133

Another Spring   136

To Do It or Not to Do It   139

Names   142

Franco, I Have So Many Things to Tell You   145

What Would He Look Like Now?   151

The Bells of Rome   154

A Memorial   159

Epilogue, 163

After Franco, 165

Dear Franco, 170

Preface

A JOURNALIST FRIEND said to me: "Send that story to the *Globe*." And not long after that, the writing of this book took off.

The first essay accepted by my local newspaper, the *Boston Globe*, was about names: as in, what do you call your new boyfriend who happens to be more than 70 years old? That boyfriend, Franco Romagnoli, later became my husband, and by the time I was ready with my next essay, he had died. Which means that all my essays since then have been about how I learned to be a widow. I wrote stories and more stories about the many changes I had to face in accepting my new status: learning to live alone again after that too-short late-in-life romance had ended for me. How do I manage to live in the same space we shared? How do I get used to being called a widow? How do I adjust to going to a movie alone again? What do I do when people ask me why I am still wearing my wedding ring? How do I get used to eating alone? How do I deal with his clothes and all the many reminiscences of our life together?

And then the letters came pouring in from readers, so many of whom thanked me for putting my feelings into words, because they felt the same way I did. They said it was such a solace to know that there were others out there who understood what they were going through. Here is what some of them wrote to me:

"I feel as though you are writing my thoughts each time I see your articles – it is good to know we are not alone."

"I have never written to an article before but after only four months as a widow, everything in the article was for me."

"Your article was a welcome read to know that I am not alone in my feelings."

"I recently read your essay on becoming a widow and it was as if I was reading a page from my own journal."

"I have experienced so many similar situations to you."

"I imagine your writing your column helps you deal with your loss, just as reading it helps me with mine."

"I am a widow of nine years and I could easily write a chapter in the book you are writing."

"I hope you complete your book on widowhood; there are so few out there that speak to women who, while strong and coping on a daily basis, are stuck."

THAT LAST LETTER was just one of the many I received urging me to write my book. And I can't tell you how many people I meet—on airplanes, at restaurants, in the drugstore, or just walking down the street—who stop and tell me how much they appreciate my articles and how much solace they have received from reading them. So writing my columns has opened up readers to me and me to them.

THIS BOOK, LEARNING *to be a* Widow, is a compilation of my essays in the *Globe,* along with many more stories that are published only here. Some are much longer than would be allowed for the space allotted by the newspaper for its column, and many follow the journeys that Franco and I made together during our brief ten years of marriage. Often, as I am sure happens with other widows, something seen or heard right now in my life will trigger a remembrance of an instance long past that my spouse and I shared. A number of my stories came to me like that.

FRIENDS AND FAMILY members helped and encouraged me during the long time it has taken me to write this accounting of my life as a widow. I still hear Marianne Jacobbi's voice in my head when she said to me: "Send that story to the *Globe*." She got me started on this path, for which I am eternally grateful. And for his careful, insightful reading and editing of some of the stories, I thank my son, Sean O'Sullivan, whom I love to pieces. He is not only one of the nicest persons I know, but also the smartest.

Joy Tutela, my agent, who has seen me through thick and thin, as they say, was responsible for the publication of Franco's childhood memoir: *The Bicycle Runner: A Memoir of Love, Loyalty and the Italian Resistance,* and Franco's and my joint venture: *Italy the Romagnoli Way: A Culinary Journal.* Joy in every way lives up to her name and has become for me a dear close friend.

Introduction

Meeting Franco And Losing Him

FOR YEARS THE operative word in my life had been "someone," or "any-one." As in, "You're so nice—how come you never meet anyone?" Or, "I wonder why, with all the divorced men around, you don't ever meet anyone?" Even better, "You'd better hurry up and meet someone, you're getting up there, you know."

I didn't have the luck of many of my divorced friends who found new husbands in a relatively short time after their divorces, or at least after a respectable period of time. I was divorced in 1974 and took almost twenty-five years to find another mate.

Then, quite unexpectedly and unbelievably, it happened. Introduced by a mutual friend, I finally met my "someone" at the age of 63, when he was just about to turn 70. Before that, during my long divorcée period, I never seemed to be able to muster the courage to become part of the "singles scene," a term that to me meant frequenting bars or partaking of a dating service. Instead, I usually spent my free time going to movies or concerts or dinners with other single women. Or sometimes I'd go out with couples who were friends from my long-ago first-marriage days, people who had managed to stay together all these years. But I never did anything as a couple, because I hadn't been part of one for such a long time.

In fact, whenever someone said "couple," the word always sounded like a totally foreign concept to me. For example, my friend Ellen and her husband have been married for more than forty years. Whenever she would tell me what they were doing or where they were going, she would say: "We're going to New York for the weekend with two other couples." Or "We're going on a cruise up to Alaska with four other couples." In her world, everybody was not only married, but married to the same people they had married forty or more years ago.

So after years and years of never meeting "anyone"—or else meeting a lot of the wrong people—when I finally found Franco, I thought for sure I'd have a huge adjustment to make. But our attraction was so strong, and we were so immediately compatible, that it took only a few days for me to go almost effortlessly from single person to member of a couple. We were inseparable from the moment we met.

I still remember vividly that cold November evening when Franco, bottle of wine in hand, appeared on my doorstep for our first date. He had bicycled in the dark the five miles from his house to mine. At the age of almost 70, he was still bicycling all over town, miles and miles at a time.

I invited him in for a drink and we sat on the couch, talking, joking, laughing, amazed at how our past lives had so often crossed and criss-crossed, both in the States and in Rome. Rome was his native city, and I had lived in Rome for seven years. Although he had moved to the States, he and his family often returned to Rome and once had lived only a few blocks from my apartment. It turned out his four children and my son got their ice cream from the same *gelateria*. We even discovered that we knew a lot of the same people, in both countries.

Conversation came so easily, it felt as if we had known each other for years. Every once in a while one of us would say, "Well, should we go out for dinner?" And then we'd immediately plunge into another incessant conversation. Finally, I said, "Why don't I just prepare a quick dinner here?" Somehow I had the audacity to offer to cook a meal for this premier Italian chef, who had had his own PBS TV show devoted to Italian cooking, *The Romagnoli's Table,* and then went on to own three restaurants and write eight cookbooks.

I decided to take a chance, knowing that everybody loved my spaghetti with zucchini and cream sauce; after all, I said to myself, you know enough about authentic Italian cuisine. But while I was cooking, I was aware of his eyes looking over my shoulder, watching my every move. Then at the table, after telling me my sauce was really good, he leaned toward me and said, "Can I hold your hand?"

"Yes," I said, feeling like a teenager, and slipped my hand into his while we finished our wine. We returned to the living room for coffee and cognac, taking up our earlier positions on the couch, and continued to recount for each other our past lives. Then suddenly, another question, "Can I kiss you?" And the next thing I knew it was morning and Franco was getting ready to bike back to his house.

*   *   *

"WHY DID IT take me such a long time to find Franco," I ask myself, "and such a short time to lose him?"

So many widows and widowers have stories to tell about the beautiful years they had with their mates and how difficult it is to live without them after forty or fifty years together.

I lost Franco after only twelve years and we were married for ten of those.

"It isn't fair," I wanted to cry out to anyone who would listen to me. It's not fair to lose someone you love so dearly after such a short time, while others have years and years together.

But then I would stop and think what it might have been like if I had met Franco when we were in our twenties or thirties and had been married for fifty years. What must it be like to live happily with someone for a long time, and suddenly not have that person next to you in bed any more? That must be hard.

IT ISN'T EASY to learn to be a widow, whatever the circumstances. Each of us bears our grief in whatever way we find we can do it. Bereavement sessions with other widows and widowers did not work for me; individual therapy could only go so far, as could talks with others who had lost a spouse. Then I began to write. Getting onto paper the reminiscences, joys, and yes, even sorrows of my life with Franco sometimes hurts but often helps—helps me to remember Franco and somehow keep him in my life.

CHAPTERS

LEARNING TO BE A WIDOW

I AM TRYING to learn how to be a widow, but it isn't going well.

Lately, I've been thinking about the various identities I've held over the years, or more precisely, my status, defined in one dictionary as that set of circumstances that characterizes a person at a given time. Until I was twenty-four years old, my status was single. In my day, you were approaching spinsterhood at the age of 24, and so I became a married woman just in the nick of time. In my late thirties, I changed my status to divorced and stayed that way for many, many years. Luckily for me, by the time I became a divorcée there was no longer a stigma attached to the term, as there had been for the generation before me. Divorce was acceptable, and it seemed everyone was doing it.

Happily, in my sixty-third year I met the love for whom I had waited almost twenty-five years, and two years later, we became husband and wife. So my status changed back to married. Couplehood suited me, and I found again the joy of sharing my life with someone. Sadly, a little more than a year ago I lost Franco, and now I am not only single again, but also a widow, a designation completely foreign to me. Although it keeps confronting me in so many contexts, the term never seems to fit.

First of all, it's the word itself. *Widow* makes me think of a woman in a long black dress, a length of black shawl trailing over her shoulders, sweeping through the dusty road of a nineteenth-century village. Or she might be looking out to sea from her perch on a widow's walk. Sometimes the word conjures up the specter of the black-widow spider. There's even a card game called widow. In printing, the last short line of a paragraph sitting by itself at the top of a page is called a widow. Meaning the one still left, alone.

Certainly, it is a term only for very, very old people. It can't be for me.

A reminder of my new status is the steady stream of official forms that confronts me. When the Watertown, Massachusetts, census form arrived, I did not fill it out because I could not bear to write that Franco was deceased. Then the U.S. census form came. The last time it showed up, ten years ago, I was happily married, and there were two of us in this household; now I can list only one. Last year, on my income-tax form, I was married filing jointly; this April I had to check the "single" box. I recently started working Friday evenings; it helps me to get out in the world as a hostess at Stellina's, my favorite restaurant. For that I had to fill out a W-4 form, and there was a choice of only two boxes to check: married or single.

There is still more paperwork that recalls my widowhood. Magazines and catalogs and invitations and political postcards and solicitations from charities keep arriving addressed to Franco. I don't know whether to write back and tell them to change the name or just let the mail keep coming, so I can still see his name as often as possible. What do I do about the museum and all those theaters and musical associations that send their notices to "Franco and Gwen"?

More new designations appear with the many appointments I am obliged to make: the Social Security office, the bank, the lawyer, the estate account, the financial manager, the health care plan. I am the executor of the estate and must file all kinds of forms and sign a lot of checks on which I write "Executrix." I have to change the bank account from "joint" to "individual." The health care company asks me to change our plan from "joint" to "survivor."

I wait in the Social Security office while the employee speaks on the phone to her superior about my new status:

"The husband is deceased," she says, "and the widow is here with me now."

I wince. Is that me? I wonder how long it takes to get used to that word.

EXTRAORDINARY MEASURES

"EXTRAORDINARY MEASURES." I could hear the intern shouting at me as I walked down the hospital hallway toward the elevator.

I turned and waited while she caught up with me.

"I don't understand," I said.

"I am asking if you want extraordinary measures for your husband."

"I know he doesn't want any extraordinary measures," I replied, "I'm sure it says so in his health care proxy. It's in his chart, isn't it?"

"Yes, it is, and you are the proxy, and that is why I am asking you."

IT WAS HALF past midnight and I could hardly stand up, exhausted from the many hours I had been living by his bedside for days and days.

"Okay, then," she said, "that's all I needed to know."

I arrived at home around 1 a.m. It had been that way for days, not only for this hospitalization but for the many that had come before. At the hospital by 8 a.m. and home around midnight. It had happened so many times in the past few years that it had become a regular part of our lives together. Taking care of Franco had become my full-time job. This time the surgeon had come up from the operating room around 11:45 p.m. and said everything had gone really well: "The procedure worked, and your husband is fine." The "procedure" had been one of the most awful

6

that he had had to endure, the inserting of a tube into his gallbladder to suck the bile out and try to get rid of the infection that had taken over inside him. The doctor would have preferred to take out the gallbladder altogether, but Franco wasn't in good enough condition to have general anesthesia. I understood that. The doctor had said, "That's okay, we do this all the time and it works quite well."

Did anybody on the staff that weekend night ever realize how sick he was, how many medical problems he had? Only later did I realize: of course, the surgeon focuses on his work, his cutting and sewing; he is the most exalted of all the doctors. If he tells you that everything went well and the patient is fine, you believe it. Especially if you aren't thinking too straight anymore about anything. But did that surgeon ever take into consideration all the other problems his patient had? Would the procedure always "work out well," no matter who your patient was?

I had just started to fall asleep about 2 a.m. when the phone rang. I recognized the voice instantly.

"I am just checking in with you again about the extraordinary measures," she said.

"Why are you calling me? Has something happened?"

"I just wanted to say that I think you should come in to the hospital."

"But, why? Please tell me what happened. Is he all right?"

Again, "I just think you should come in right away."

In fifteen minutes I was at my doorway waiting for the taxi (at least I knew enough not to drive). It didn't come as quickly as I had hoped. I stood there shivering; it was Monday morning, December 15, and there was a cold and biting wind. We arrived at the hospital around three, and I went straight up to the fourteenth floor.

As I approached his room, I saw that it was filled with people. When I had left, there had been just one nurse. Now there were many people I had never seen before. It was a room for two patients, and the curtain between them had been pulled shut. I passed the bed of the other patient and stopped. Strapped to Franco's face was a huge plastic cup that was connected to oxygen from the wall outlet; he was gasping, and everyone around him was looking, touching, adjusting tubes and arranging various pieces of equipment. Franco looked awful, pale and straining for breath.

"What is that?" I cried.

"It is a large special mask to help him breathe," somebody said.

I ran to his side and sat next to him.

"Franco," I called, "Franco." He did not turn toward me. He did not move.

"Doesn't he hear me?" I asked whoever was next to me.

"He is unconscious," the nurse said.

"Unconscious! How can that be? The doctor told me everything went well."

"He began to have trouble breathing."

I leaned as close as I could and kept shouting, "Franco, Franco, don't you hear me?"

"They say that a patient in this state can hear when you talk to them, so you should keep on talking," said somebody in a white coat.

In this state? I kept talking and hugging and kissing him, but he never moved. Then in an instant, I saw that he had stopped gasping, he just stopped.

"He stopped breathing." I turned to someone else in a white coat.

Then they asked me to move out of the way, but I knew already.

MORE THAN A year has passed, and I still can't get it out of my head—if only, if only somebody, even that intern who kept interrogating me, or our regular doctor or somebody—if only someone had talked to me, I could have been prepared. She should have told me why she was constantly asking me about extraordinary measures. Franco had been in the hospital so many times—kidney biopsy, kidney failure, dialysis, a kidney transplant, a failure of that kidney, then back on dialysis, peritoneal dialysis at home, infections, then congestive heart failure—and each time someone would ask about the health care proxy and extraordinary measures in that perfunctory we-are-required-by-law-to-ask manner. So how was I to know that this time was to be different from all the others? Why didn't that intern say right then and there, "I think you should stay; he is very sick, and we can't be sure he will live."

I would have known not to go home that night from the hospital. He had still been conscious when I left; he had said goodnight to me. I could have had him for three more hours.

*   *   *

THEY TELL YOU to move away and then they take you out of the room. You, the only person who really cares about the patient, you have to leave while all the others who don't even know him, they get to stay. I know what they're doing, though; I am picturing it the whole time while I'm out in the hall, trying to hold myself up against the wall. They are taking that horrible mask off of his face, they are taking that bloody tube out of his side where they had put it for the operation, they are doing something with that thing in his stomach they called a "port" where we had to attach the dialysis tubes, they are cleaning him up so he is presentable to me. Are they closing his eyes?

I have to wait in the hallway with the lovely blond nurse, the one Franco called "my angel," the only one who had been with him when I left him earlier. I felt my knees giving way; even leaning against the wall, my knees gave way. The angel held me up as best she could.

"Would you like to call somebody?" she asked.

"Call somebody? Yes, I guess I need to call somebody."

It was four o'clock in the morning that Monday, December 15, that day so near to Christmas. All I could think of was my son, Sean, in Columbus, Ohio. *I'll have to call him. I'll have to call Franco's kids, too.* My heart sank at the thought of what I was going to have to say to all these people.

"I'll call my friend Erica," I said at last, and tried to remember how the cell phone worked.

Her number rang and rang and rang until finally the answering machine came on. I didn't know what to do—leave a message, at four in the morning when people were asleep? What if she never got it until the daylight hours? Finally, I said, "This is Gwen. If you get this message, can you please call me on my cell phone." And then I called back again, and Erica answered; the phone had woken her. "I'll come right away," she said.

Then they let me go back into his room. He was neatly covered with a sheet, and all the tubes and machines and masks and needles and beeping things were gone. He was so pale, his eyes closed. I went to hug him, and he was already cold. How could that be, so fast?

Somebody approached my elbow as I sat on the bed.

"Do you know what funeral home to call?"

Already, the funeral home?

"If you just give me the name, I will call them and they will come and they will take care of everything."

What is everything?

"They will take his body away to their place and make all the arrangements for death certificates, for funeral services, everything you want, so you don't have to think about it. But they must come soon or your husband's body will be taken to the hospital morgue."

Morgue? I'd only seen that on TV shows. I had never been sure there really was such a thing, but now I know there is, right there in the bowels of the building where I was standing.

"Yes, I know the funeral home, because Franco told me he used it when his wife died—his first wife."

"I will call them; you don't have to worry about a thing."

And all I could think of was Sean. He'd so often say to me: "What, me worry?" teasing me about that *Mad* magazine guy. He knows that I worry even when absolutely nothing is happening....

ERICA APPEARS AT the door and I run to hug her. She looks at Franco, so quietly lying there—is he peaceful, should I say peacefully lying there?—and tears come into her eyes. She and her husband, David, live in our same condo building and are our good friends. I am so grateful she is there, at such an ungodly hour.

Then, I can tell, they are wanting us to go away. All sorts of medical and administrative people will now take over, a funeral director will come. Just another dead person for them. Happens every day. He belongs to them now, not to me any more. I will not ever see Franco again.

FINDING FRANCO'S MANUSCRIPT

THE POSTMAN HANDED me the package from the publisher in the late afternoon of December 15. It contained the final galleys of the memoir that Franco had been working on for so long, about his childhood in Rome during Mussolini's fascist regime. Franco had died just twelve hours earlier.

I had laid eyes on a much older version of that manuscript in 1996, a few weeks after Franco and I met. A mutual friend had introduced us and we immediately became inseparable. Even though we had just met, I had known about Franco for years—from his popular cooking show on PBS and his restaurant, The Romagnolis' Table, in Faneuil Hall in Boston. In fact, because I used to live in Italy, I would eat there often and had bought several of Franco's cookbooks.

I first spied the manuscript when Franco had opened the bottom drawer of his desk, and I saw a large sheaf of papers titled *Over Here.*

"What's that?" I asked.

"Oh," said Franco with a sigh of resignation, "that's a manuscript I've been working on forever, about growing up in Italy during the war. It's seen lots of publishers who have all said no, so I've given up on it."

A few weeks later, on our first trip together to the island of Vieques, I spent languid days in a hammock reading his pages. I loved it and told him we had to get it published.

"It's all yours," said Franco.

I contacted his longtime literary agent, who had also given up after having received numerous letters full of high praise from publishers who then turned the book down because it wasn't for "their market." Thus began my foray into the mysterious world of publishing. A short time after Franco and I married, I sought out agents and editors, all of whom loved it but said it needed work, and certainly a new title. "Nobody will know what *Over Here* means," they said. But for Franco it had great meaning, because the American soldiers marching into Rome were singing the old World War I song "Over There" while he said to himself, "For me it's 'Over Here,' in Italy where I live."

Months and years passed while Franco rewrote and edited. And then, suddenly, Franco became ill and was diagnosed with kidney disease, a problem that would plague us for the rest of our days together. We had known that our vows—in sickness and in health—could mean more of the former because of our ages, but it had never occurred to us that sickness would come so soon.

As time went by, Franco went on dialysis, a transplant failed, he got sicker. Meanwhile, I plodded ahead looking for a home for his book. By lucky chance, I was introduced to Joy, another agent, who loved the manuscript, accepted it, and gave it a new title. She was vigorous and unrelenting, advising further rewriting. Franco worked with her until he pronounced he had achieved the final version.

Eventually we learned how to do Franco's kidney treatment at home. We would hook him up each evening to a machine that would do the dialysis for him all night. Then in the morning, we'd unhook it and start as normal a day as we could. Before turning it off, I would write down the numbers it showed, go downstairs, and transcribe them in my faithful "kidney book." These numbers would tell us how Franco was doing that day.

Just about that time, Joy announced she had at last found a publisher.

The day after the postman came, I woke up and Franco wasn't there beside me. The machine stood silent in the corner, perched on the table he had made for it. My pad of paper lay on the bedside table, but there were no numbers to write down.

I didn't know how to start the day without the numbers.

Downstairs I looked over at the rolltop desk and expected to see him sitting there at his computer, tapping away with two fingers, as always. Perhaps he's started that book about his time as a chef, or he's typing out his latest recipe or short story, or working on still another version of the memoir.

That memoir forms the bookends of our life together. Maybe, I think, if it had never been finished, he'd still be here with me.

THE FIRST WEEK

THE THING I want most is for nothing to happen, nobody to call me, nobody to write me or knock on the door—except of course for Sean, my sweet, caring son. I can't even remember when I made the call to him out there in Ohio—would it have been 4 a.m., or did I wait for a more respectable hour, like six? Whatever it was, the moment he heard my voice, I heard him say, "Mom, I'll be right there." And by afternoon, he was and stayed with me all week. He's a professor at Ohio State, and I don't know if he had to cancel all his classes; all I know is, I am so thankful for Sean.

I just want to stay inside and wait for the evening to come; it gets dark early, it's December. I'll have my glass of wine and go to bed, get under the covers and try not to think too much. Instead, they don't let you do that. You have things to do, you have appointments to keep, every single day: Sean and I must go to the undertaker's place the very next day, because he needs to know what to do with the body ... what a terrible thing to have to think of. I know that Franco wanted to be cremated, but the more I picture him burning up in some furnace somewhere, the more I hesitate. Would it be better to be packed into a box and put under the ground and be eaten by worms? No, do what he wanted and try not to think about it. Here, says the undertaker, here are ten copies of the death certificate. The death certificate? How did they do that so quickly? And for the first time, I find out what they say he died of, three things, in order from most recent to last. Sepsis? Nobody told me sepsis. But then I wasn't even there when some doctor wrote this thing up. You must have several copies, the funeral director says, because you will need them for many, many things. Oh, I will?

Then we have to go to the cemetery guy because he needs to know what to do, too. He will take care of the cremating right there at Mount Auburn Cemetery, that beautiful place where Franco and I took so many walks, where he took so many gorgeous photos.

Sean once again puts me in the passenger seat of the car and this time drives me to the lawyer's office. For his estate, I am the executrix; some think that's a funny name. The lawyer needs some death certificates to file in court, he needs Social Security numbers, he needs lists of assets, he needs …

AND THEN SOMEONE was knocking on my door. I didn't know what people did when there is a death. I had never lived in a big apartment building before, so I didn't know what people did when somebody died right there in the same building. I know now: They come to your door laden with food and flowers and hugs. It all made me remember the couple I had interviewed for my erstwhile book, *Gray Love,* about people who meet later in life and fall in love. The wife had been divorced for a while, but the man had just been widowed, like Franco and me. The two had known each other in a circle of mutual friends in their town, and it seemed as if this new widower would be a good catch. So, the wife told me she didn't want to go round to his house too soon, brisket in hand, since it might appear she was after him. So she waited what she hoped was a respectable time to go visit him. Apparently it worked, because now they are married to each other.

For me, there was no such thing as having to wait. The very first morning, my close friend Ginnie stayed with me all day until Sean got there. Sweet, kind Ginnie, who just happened to phone me because she knew that Franco had been in the hospital on the weekend. She was wondering how he was doing and if he might be coming back home soon. She was there with me within a half hour.

A neighbor came with a whole roast chicken; people kept calling ... from Rome, from Washington, from California—how did they know? It was the very next day. Florists arrived delivering cut flowers and plants, and soon the room became so filled with them, I didn't have enough vases. People just kept talking to me and talking to me, on the phone, at the door, in the room, and I would respond as if nothing new had happened.

Only later on did I learn that you cannot grieve—they just don't let you grieve—that first week, or second week, or more. They keep you busy with appointments that have to be kept, events that have to be planned, like the service, dividing up the address book, so different people get assigned to calling different people with the news. Franco's sister in Rome, our old dear friends all over the country....

After that rush, after all the plans had been made, that was when the anxiety attacks started happening, the ones where my legs would give out and I'd find myself leaning against the nearest wall. The Italian shop where Sean took me, and then had to hold me up when the rush of tears came out of nowhere and my knees buckled, just looking at the Italian food and hearing Franco say to me: "Don't buy those big zucchini; only the small ones are good." Sean had taken me out to Columbus with him so I could have Christmas with him and Hannah, and little Rory, then 5, and Eve, only 2. What better place for me to be, there was none.

I had to go back home, though, in the new year of 2009. Plans were being made for the memorial service, to be held on his birthday, February 1, and invitations needed to be sent, things had to be organized for the use of the chapel, more friends had to be called. More visits to the lawyer, to the bank, to the Social Security office ... now I remember how I kept busy those first months after his death. When it's all done, that's when you're left alone again. That's when the hardest part begins.

The evenings, too many of them, I spend waiting to get in bed. The evening news we always watched together, a couple of glasses of pinot grigio, maybe a movie or a book. I can't wait to get under the covers again. Another day is finished. How can it be, after all these years, that the best time of my life is just being in bed? I get into the bed and stretch out my arm to touch the sheet on the other side of the bed; my hand moves round and round searching for some sign of him. The dialysis machine is gone, but the table he made by hand is still there, full of books. And then I spy something I hadn't seen for so long—the mirror he had nailed to the wall across from the machine so he would be able to read the numbers, just to assure himself everything was under control. And I can even smile, remembering how long it took me to position the mirror in just the right spot while he lay on the bed, saying, "Now it's too low, now it's too much to the right, no, it's worse than it was before, there, you've almost got it, all right, let's give it up for now and try again later."

Then there was the morning I woke up and finally knew he would never be next to me in bed again, that this time he really wasn't going to come home from the hospital, that this time was different.

DEVIL IN A BLUE DRESS

With the TV remote in hand, I am scrolling through the Guide section, looking at the various channels that show movies, as I do most evenings when I am at home. If a movie I want to see is on at a reasonable hour, I might watch it then, but often the ones I like are on too late, so I record them to watch another time. Suddenly, this evening *Devil in a Blue Dress*, with Denzel Washington, pops up on HBO, and my mind flashes back to the first week I knew Franco.

It was a Friday, our fifth date, which occurred on the fifth day after I had met him. It was the Monday just before that when he had first appeared on my doorstep with a bottle of wine in hand. From that moment, we were together every day. It seemed so completely natural, as if we were always meant to be together anyway, so why wait around to have a date the next week? Why wait? When you finally meet the right man this late in life, there is no time to lose. We couldn't waste a single minute.

This was our first movie date. He arrived at my house around 4 p.m. so we could get to the Arlington theater by four-thirty, senior-citizen time, to see *Devil in a Blue Dress*. It was a mystery/detective story, and it was then that I learned how much Franco loved to read detective stories. We were just about out the door when my phone rang. It was Hannah, my son's girlfriend, later, happily, to become my daughter-in-law.

"Hi, Hannah, I can't talk too long because I'm about to go out to a movie."

"Who with?" she asked immediately.

"Oh, just a friend."

"What friend?"

"Oh, you don't know who it is."

"You're going out with a man, aren't you?"

I should have known: Hannah is uncanny. How does she do this, I asked myself?

"How could you possibly know whether I am or not?" I said, sending glances back and forth to Franco, my eyes saying, *How does she know this?*

"I don't know, I can just tell—there is something different in your voice."

"What could be different? I often go to the movies with friends."

"I sense something, I just sense, this is different...."

"Okay, okay," I finally relented. "I am going to see *Devil in a Blue Dress* with a man."

"Who is it? C'mon, who?"

"I'm not telling. I really am in a hurry or we will miss the show."

Then it started: "I'll just ask what field he is in, and then you have to answer yes or no."

She started down her list: the law, medicine, engineering, computers, academia, and I can't remember how many others.

And at last, "Food!"

I was silent for a moment, still trying to avoid this conversation. I mean, I had only known Franco for five days now, and I had been thinking I'd wait a few more days before notifying the world. But Hannah was relentless.

"I know, I know," she shouted, "it's Franco Romagnoli."

*   *   *

FRANCO AND I went to the movies often and watched movies on TV a lot, too. Any mystery story that came along, he would want to see. Any Italian movie, of course, we had to go, both of us starved for movies from Italy. For other choices, we were not always in sync about what to see. For Franco movie-going was entertainment; it was not meant to be a serious occupation. A favorite for him would be watching the Three Stooges, whose movies he had first seen in Italy after the war. He wanted to laugh and have a good time. I wanted to laugh and have a good time, too, but I also liked serious movies, about tragedy or romance and complications. And I was not at all bothered by ambiguous endings, because then you'd have to think more about what you had seen. Like many French movies that leave you hanging at the end, you are supposed to contemplate that movie and discuss it with friends.

An ambiguous ending to a movie was for Franco totally unacceptable. Things needed to be tied up; films, like novels, had to have a beginning, a middle, and an end that was conclusive. Not necessarily happy; it could be sad if that was called for, but it had to leave you satisfied.

"Otherwise, what's the point?" he'd say. "After all, we are going to the movies for entertainment, not to have to think."

The subject that my son, Sean, happens to teach at Ohio State is film, and he is a great proponent of ambiguity. He and Franco loved and respected each other: They could speak in Italian with each other, they could talk about recipes and many other things. But the topic of cinema was their favorite. They could discuss ad infinitum the positive and negative features of movies, Franco usually focusing on the beauty or skill of the cinematography. He had been, after all, a filmmaker for many years, and a photographer as well. Beauty was fine for Sean: after all, how could one criticize beauty? But convolution was interesting; plot twists were intriguing. *Memento* was a favorite film of Sean's, one he had studied and taught—the film that went backward and took at least three viewings to figure out, if even that was enough.

I remember the time *Memento* came up on one of those TV movie channels, and I said to Franco: "We should watch this again, maybe we'll figure it out this time."

"Oh please, please," begged Franco, "do not make me watch *Memento* ever again!"

Okay, we don't have to watch *Memento* again, but I do have to watch *Devil in a Blue Dress* once again tonight. The movie always brings back to mind that Friday date with Franco and the prescient phone call from Hannah. I haven't forgotten a word of it.

THOSE WRETCHED TV ADS

UH-OH, THERE'S ANOTHER one of those ads on TV for Celebrex. And there is the tiny print running underneath with a voice saying in a rapid staccato pace words that are mostly incomprehensible. I catch some of them: "If you have kidney disease or think you have kidney disease, ask your doctor whether Celebrex is right for you. Side effects may include…" and on and on and on; the words keep coming that nobody can understand.

KIDNEY DISEASE!

Why is it that kidney disease keeps coming up in so many drug commercials? "Do not take this medicine if you have kidney disease," over and over again.

Each time I hear those words, my heart skips a beat and I go back to remembering:

THOSE LEGS.

I'll never forget the first time I laid eyes on those legs. They were spectacular: thin and wiry, without even a centimeter of fat. They were sixty-nine-year-old legs, but they could have belonged to an eighteen-year-old, so taut and slim and muscular. While my legs had begun to show a little advanced-age flab in the thighs, Franco had none. *How does he do it,* I'd wonder?

IT CAME SO suddenly and unexpectedly, the news that would forever change our lives.

We were sitting on the patio in the backyard on July 15, 2001, having a late-afternoon drink. I remember well that date, because it was the birthday of my father, who had died only a few years earlier at the age of 101.

Franco was, as usual, tilting back on one of the garden chairs with his legs propped against another chair. I happened to glance over in his direction and suddenly noticed that the ankles of those normally superb, reed-thin legs were swollen and bloated out of all proportion.

Franco was a few years older than I, and despite the existence of a somewhat protruding *pancia* (for an Italian a prominent stomach indicates affluence, or so Franco always said), he was in excellent physical health, those legs as trim as an athlete's. And so it was all the more strange—even alarming—to notice the huge swelling of those perfect limbs. Franco had not noticed at all or even felt anything different. When I approached to take a closer look, he untilted his chair and looked down. He was as surprised as I was. He didn't feel anything, he said, no pain, no discomfort, no change at all. I pressed my index finger into his lower calf, and when I withdrew my finger, a huge indentation remained in his skin. Isn't this odd, we said.

WE CALL THE doctor's office to describe the circumstances, and the word comes back from the secretary that we should come in the very next day. Getting an appointment that quickly makes us start to worry. Why the hurry? What could this be?

Franco's doctor is a lovely young woman named Dr. Roberts (he always seemed to have young women doctors and we ended up having a lot more in the years ahead) who takes one look at the legs and orders blood tests.

"We can't be sure," she says, "but swelling like this is often an indication that something could be wrong with the kidneys. It's called edema; most likely your body is retaining liquid that should have been expelled. And that's what the kidneys do. We should know something by tomorrow."

Then comes the usual questionnaire with all those queries about your health background from the time you were born, including, "Is there any kidney disease in your family?"

"Not that I know of," Franco writes. "All I know about my family is that everyone is hard of hearing."

Except of course, as Franco and I knew well, if you ask Italians, "*Come state?*" ("How are you?"), they are apt to tell you exactly how they are, with more details about their bodies than you would ever want to know. Whereas we in America might say, "Fine, thanks," even if we are not fine at all, Italians love to tell you how they really are. Except for one thing: No one wants to give a name to the really bad diseases. Even today they will not say "*cancro*" if someone is sick or has died of cancer; instead they will say "*quella brutta malattia,*" ("that nasty sickness"), and everyone knows what it is. So it can sometimes be hard to say whether somebody in your family ever had the disease you now have, because the name might never have been uttered.

Dr. Roberts prescribes Lasix, a diuretic that makes a person pee a lot and thus helps reduce the swelling. Next day, we get the results of the blood tests, which unfortunately do show that those kidneys aren't working the way they are supposed to. Dr. Roberts shows us a page full of figures indicating what's happening in Franco's blood. This piece of paper is the beginning of our journey through the meaning of numbers, what they represent, what number they are supposed to be, but unfortunately are not, what numbers may be good and which are bad, are they going up when they should go down, or vice versa. Words never before known to us begin that day to take over our whole lives: creatinine, serum albumin, hemoglobin, hematocrit, proteinuria, glucose, edema, neuropathy, immunoproteins, prothrombin time, humulin insulin, potassium level, phosphorous level, hypoglycemia....

Especially *creatinine*: I had never heard the word before, but from that date on I would say it every day of my life. You always want that number to go down, and you cringe if you hear it went up, even a tiny percentage point. It is the marker of the filtering ability of the kidney; it measures the amount of toxins the kidney excretes out of the blood, and the ideal number is something around 0.6. Franco's number is 2.2 and it needs to come down, but, the doctor tells us, kidneys fail gradually, never suddenly, and some time will pass before the number becomes alarming. When to worry? The number 8.

I think about one of Sean's favorite movie directors, Peter Greenaway, and his film *Drowning by Numbers*. We are about to embark on such a drama.

Dr. Roberts tells us that Franco will need a biopsy to know just exactly what the diagnosis is. It seems there are a lot of different problems a kidney can have, and we need to know what our problem is so the right treatment can be prescribed. And "our" problem it turned out to be.

"Why me?" asked Franco of no one at all.

We were lying in bed that night, talking about the blood-test results and trying to make sense of what had just happened. In a matter of only two days, we had gone from thinking we were in good health to knowing that a serious illness had just made its way into our lives.

Okay, your serum protein is abnormal, the albumin is much too low, only half as normal as it should be, blood counts and platelets are okay; and there isn't any hepatitis or any other disease. So that's two good things, except that there were 22 grams of protein in the urine—a very big amount. And then there's the creatinine.

And so, with this smattering of information, began the course of our knowledge of the kidney, as we learned every tiny detail about the function and operation of this very important organ. In the ensuing years, I filled up two entire notebooks with every doctor's visit, the numbers from every test, and collected a file full of brochures about kidneys and their function.

We were just beginning our odyssey into the realm of nephrology.

BICYCLING

It is early September and I am at the Cape, staying at my niece's house for a few days. Each morning, as I have done every year when I visit, I take my hour walk along the paths by the ocean. This morning is one of those perfect cloudless days, just about the best time of year to be on Cape Cod.

As I walk along, earphones firmly planted on my ears and into my iPod, where Rachmaninoff's Third Piano Concerto is playing, a bicycle suddenly passes me on the right. A middle-aged man decked out in typical bike-riding attire (helmet, of course; rubberized knee-length shorts; Lance Armstrong T-shirt) waves at me. A few seconds pass and then the wife, properly clothed and helmeted, leaning over, a serious bike rider. She, too, waves. Then another man … and I just know that there will be a woman right after him, and there is. A third man passes next, surely part of a couple … and not more than a few seconds later, she comes by and waves. That's three couples all in a row. That is the way it used to be for Franco and me, he first, with me a few seconds later. Now I can't even remember what happened to my bike.

We bicycled together all the time. Not long after I moved into his house, Franco bought me a beautiful new bike, having made the decision that repairing my old one would be a hopeless task—even for him, the preeminent tinkerer. We would start from his house, which was on a hill, glide down, and then pedal onto the sidewalks of the main street. He could outdo me anytime, but we both felt wary enough of Boston drivers to stay on the sidewalk, never sure if that was illegal or not. We rode along the Charles River on pathways that took us almost to Waltham. We talked of getting a tandem. Then on the way back, he could get all the way up the hill to our house on his bike, but I never could. Humiliated, about halfway up (or maybe less) I would have to get off and walk. "How can you do that?" I would marvel. He was seventy-two years old.

We walked a lot, too. We walked long distances along the river, and he could never understand why he could walk faster than I could. He'd say, "You are tall and have those long, long legs—why do you take such short steps?" In all my life, nobody had ever said that to me before. I began to pay attention to my stride, taking much longer steps, but he could still go faster.

Franco was a champion swimmer, too. When he was fifteen years old, right in the middle of World War II, he and his swimming colleagues traveled from Rome to Torino to compete in a swimming match. Mussolini always made a big deal about strong bodies, so sporting events had to continue even while bombs were falling all over Italy. Franco won his match and a gold medal. Luckily his team had left the pool and were outside on the street just before the bomb fell on the gymnasium.

He could easily outdo me in the swimming pool. When we went swimming together, he still had the stamina to go back and forth countless times doing the breaststroke. For me, that took too much breath and too much energy. I was a hopeless swimmer with any stroke. He taught me how to do the crawl correctly and then would critique my form. Getting better all the time, he'd say.

It took only three years of our lives together for all this to be reversed. That time we took a walk along Mount Auburn Street and had to turn back after only a few blocks because he was out of breath. We sat down for a few minutes on the stone wall along the street in front of the church, and then he asked if I could go and get the car, come back, and pick him up.

*   *   *

Dr. Roberts was what is now called a PCP. That always sounds to me like a substance forbidden for use by the Environmental Protection Agency, it's so close to "PCBs." But it really stands for primary care physician. Some of us who are too old to change keep calling our doctors just "doctor" or maybe "principal doctor." It used to be your internist, but nowadays that word sounds as if it is a doctor who only deals with your innards. Regardless of what appellation Dr. Roberts used, she soon made it clear that the situation was serious enough for us to be referred to a kidney specialist, a nephrologist, as soon as possible.

Two weeks later we are in the waiting room of one Dr. Segall, a kindly gentleman who greets us with "And how are *youuu?*" with an upswing on the word "you."

He asks us to sit down and begins to explain in a most methodical way everything there is to know about the kidney, thankfully using words that are as close as a physician can get to making a layperson understand. The kidneys are like filters, he explain. Imagine these two organs covered by mesh. Basically, all the bad stuff that is left over in your body after you eat goes down to the kidneys which in turn filter all the bile out of your body but keep all the good stuff in. So things that our bodies need, like protein, will stay in. When that mesh starts to tear or fall apart, the good things go out along with the bad. And when your body starts to lose protein and begins to retain the bad liquid, your limbs will start to swell. Salt in your body makes you swell, too, so it's of great importance not to eat much salt. Now we have to find out just which kidney disease we have here, because, as it turns out, there are many causes for the kidney not to function properly. For that, Franco will need a kidney biopsy.

But first, Dr. Segall orders an ultrasound of both Franco's bladder and his kidneys. That happens right away at that first visit, and the results come right back. All normal! Ah, some good news for us to dwell on, at least until the biopsy which will happen ten days later. That is considered a real operation, so you need to go through all that pre-op testing stuff. More blood tests, more blood-pressure testing, the usual vital signs, long questionnaires to fill out, discussions with the anesthesiologist. Basically, a half-day's mission.

The day for the biopsy arrives: it's August 16, 2001. Franco has to go under general anesthesia, and then the surgeon will insert a long, thick needle into his back to pull out a little tissue from a kidney. Our two kidneys are located in our backs, just a little lower than our waists, one on each side of our spine, just behind the ribs. I ask the surgeon why he doesn't have to take tissue from both of them, but he says one is enough. Whenever you get a disease in your kidney, usually both of them get it, we are told. What's wrong with one is wrong with both. We won't know for a day or two because the tissue will have to be sent to the pathologist, and then on to still another pathologist to be sure the first one got the right diagnosis.

The word that comes back from both pathologists is: *membranous.* That is kidney shorthand for what turned out to be Franco's diagnosis. The whole name is *membranous glomerulo nephropathy.*

With the seemingly endless questions from a seemingly endless array of doctors, nurses, pharmacists, physician assistants, nurse practitioners, surgeons, we soon became so familiar with our circumstances that before they even asked, we could say, "Franco has membranous."

On the biopsy report, we see there is written the acronym ESRD. "What is that?" we both ask. It stands for End Stage Renal Disease, we are told.

My heart leaps out of my chest. End stage?

"Why is it called end stage if it has just begun?" I ask Dr. Segall.

And he tells us that all kidney disease is called ESRD because when the kidneys get this bad it means that sooner or later they are going to fail.

AN EMPTY SPACE

I LOOK AROUND me and see a very large living room.

This condo I live in never used to seem so big. In fact, it once seemed much too small for two people. Seven years ago, when we decided it was time to move out of our big Victorian house and leave snow shoveling and lawn mowing to someone else, Franco and I looked at many condos and my comment about every one of them was: "It's too small."

Now I rattle around in this place from one end to the other. There are too many choices: I can sit in that chair by the window or on the small sofa across the room or on any part of the big couch that I want to, because Franco is no longer sitting in his spot next to me. I can sit at the dining table or never sit there at all. I can keep sleeping on my side of the bed, or sometimes sleep on his, or even in the middle. There is no one to share this space with now.

What single person needs three bathrooms? The condo we chose happens to be a duplex, with one bathroom downstairs and one each for the two bedrooms upstairs. When Franco was here and very ill, we were glad to have the one downstairs, so he didn't have to climb the stairs. We had so much bathroom equipment then that we might have qualified for a rest home: the raised toilet seat, the commode in the middle of the bedroom (just in case), the walker to get back and forth to the bathroom. I gave all those things to the nursing home up the street. Now I feel as if I am in the VIP suite of some fancy hotel with an overload of amenities.

And then there is the kitchen, the very same that made me say to Franco, when we first looked at the condo: "How are you ever going to cook anything in this place?"

We had given up his enormous well-equipped kitchen, set in a greenhouse with floor-to-ceiling windows and loads of flowering plants. Many recipes had been tested in that gorgeous kitchen for Franco's show on WGBH, called *The Romagnoli's Table*—the very first television show on Italian food. Many videos had been shot in that kitchen on subjects such as how to make pasta by hand, a *timbalo* or Bolognese sauce, and many other splendid Italian dishes.

This tiny excuse for a kitchen doesn't even have a gas stove, because there is only electricity in this building. Totally unacceptable for a real cook. We both learned to cook on it anyway, because we had to. Now it sits there practically unused. Every once in a while, I get up the courage to invite friends to dinner and can't remember which cabinet contains the pots and pans I need.

"Why not try to make this place your own?" some friends say. "Move the furniture around, or buy new things. Paint each room a different color. Put new pictures on the walls."

"I don't think I'm ready for that," I reply. "Maybe later."

And, I think, *what is "my own" anyway?* Even though I was already in my sixties when I met Franco, I had just recently bought and moved into the only house I had ever owned. "His own" was the gorgeous Victorian in which he had resided for forty years. After we decided to live together, we each wrote down what we thought were the pros and cons of living in his house or my house. I found that piece of paper the other day, still in my desk drawer: among the pros for me was that my house was right near the Red Line subway stop, and that I had just about finished fixing it up so it would become the way I wanted it to be. Franco didn't need to write down many pros for his house; it was clearly more beautiful, with all its

Victorian detail intact, and that enormous kitchen with all that history about his cooking show. But the *pièce de résistance* came when I stayed at his house for the weekend and he made a fire in the bedroom fireplace. It was the first time in my life I had ever seen a house that had a fireplace in the bedroom, let alone one that really worked. The sheet of paper with the pros and cons on it suddenly became unnecessary, and a few months later I moved in with Franco.

This condo is the only place we lived in that was truly "ours."

I LIKE TO look around and know that Franco would still find it a familiar place, to look at the paintings and photographs that we looked at together in the places they've always been ... watching that flat-screen television that I bought on a whim, the one he teased me about because it was so big, but soon was quite happy to watch ... the couch in the exact same place we sat on it together ... the terrace we looked out on, with the same flowers planted in the same pots that Franco first planted them in.

And no matter what part of the bed I sleep on at night, I still reach out to the other side and move my hand around the sheet, longing to find him there beside me.

TRAVELING WITH LASIX

EILEEN AND DAN have just returned from their trip to Toronto to celebrate Dan's eightieth birthday. Dan didn't feel up to going too far away, like to Israel, as they'd planned much earlier, but they wanted to travel somewhere. Maybe just to show they could still do it. They tell me how big the city is, so much larger than they had expected, and how they drove to Stratford and saw three plays. I want to hear all about it. I've never been to Toronto, or to Stratford, but then, as they tell me the details, I realize I really don't want to hear about their trip. I don't want to picture them together on an airplane, holding hands, or perhaps her fingers pressing into his arm, as I used to with Franco because I was always afraid when the plane was taking off. Or think of them staying in a beautiful room in a nice hotel, eating dinner together, sleeping together in the same bed, getting up in the morning, having breakfast together, going out on the streets of the city, arm in arm. I can picture them moving ever so slowly, seeing Dan with his stooped shoulders and feeble gait.

As they tell me about their adventures, I realize I'd much rather think of the trips Franco and I took together. Especially that first trip we took after we heard the diagnosis of kidney disease, that summer of 2001. We'd done lots of traveling before that, but this was different. Like Dan, Franco didn't have the stamina he'd once had. Our plan was to travel all over Italy, from top to toe, researching the book we were writing together about the less-traveled parts of the country. Dr. Segall wasn't sure we should go.

We were lucky, we told him, to have something fun and uplifting to look forward to, to help take our minds off the state of our health for a while. We had just gotten the news that a publisher was interested in the book we wanted to call *Travels with My Fork: Off the Eaten Path in Italy.* It was to be a compilation of articles we each had written before we met, about the parts of Italy we each knew particularly well. And now we would add all the new ones we would write together. Each chapter would be about a lesser-known place in Italy, off-the-beaten-track spots where fewer tourists go, starting from the northernmost Alps all the way down to Sicily and beyond. And, of course, there would be an emphasis on the food in those areas, along with recipes.

I had lived in the early 1960s in Puglia, which at that time pretty much nobody outside of Italy had even heard of. Now it's become quite fashionable for Americans to visit the famous *trulli* cone houses of Alberobello or the posh new *agri-turismi* centers, or take bicycle tours along the country roads lined with the oldest, most magnificent olive trees I had ever seen. But when I first laid eyes on Bari, the principal city where I lived, or any of the small towns in the region, I never once heard a word of English uttered by anybody. That's why it was easy for me to get a job teaching English to adult Italians, who had been forbidden during Fascism to learn the language in school. So I could write with knowledge about those once-unknown places.

Franco was born and grew up in Rome, but spent his childhood summers in a little town in the region called Le Marche, where his grandfather had a farm. Later he lived on the mountain called Monte San Vicino, hiding out among the partisan fighters toward the end of World War II. He, of course, knew many more hidden spots than I did, but together we put our thoughts and words into a proposal for this book, and started making plans for a nice long trip to Italy to do our research.

Then came September 11th.

Franco was at the gym, swimming. He was feeling pretty good. I was in the living room, watching TV of course, and constantly running out into the driveway to see if he was on his way home. He was riding his bike, and finally I heard him coming up the street.... *He doesn't know.*

Like everyone else, we spent the next days unable to take our eyes off the TV set.

Then back to still another appointment with Dr. Segall.

"What about Italy?" we asked.

"Well, I guess it will be okay," he said, "but you will have to be on medication. I will prescribe Lasix to help keep the kidneys working, making you piss as much as possible. And Prednisone, a steroid. But you will have to be strict about the dosage you take and the schedule you are on. You will have to keep track of everything in a notebook I will give you. When you come back, you will show it to me, and we will do more tests."

Prednisone, the one I called the miracle drug, I knew had to be taken in decreasing doses because it is such a powerful medicine. And I have always been a most proficient notetaker.

Now we had two big worries to overcome: Not just the state of Franco's health, but also the fear of flying ... anywhere. We thought and thought about it, and finally decided that November 2001 just might be one of the safest times to travel. And so, with Dr. Segall's reluctant approval, we bought our tickets. On November 2, armed with a two-month supply of Prednisone and Lasix, we flew from Boston to Milano on an uneventful and sparsely populated Alitalia flight. Even the weather cooperated. As we approached Malpensa, we saw the usual Milanese fog shrouding the airport, but as soon as we landed, the sun came out and stayed that way for almost our whole two-month trip. We were back in Italy.

Our first stop was Lago di Orta, which Franco called "the Cinderella of the Lakes" because it is much overshadowed by the fame of Lakes Garda, Como, and Maggiore, the last of which is located just a bit east of Orta. We got ourselves installed in a gorgeous hotel with picture windows looking right out onto the swan-filled lake, and called Franco's sister in Rome.

"*Dove siete?*" Where are you? she asked.

"Orta," Franco replied.

"*Dove? Orte?*" she asked, mentioning a small town that is hardly more than a railroad junction near Orvieto, barely an hour from Rome.

"No, Lago di Ort-a, up north!"

"*Mai sentito.*" Never heard of it.

Well, we decided, if Mirella, who is quite well traveled, had never heard of Orta, we were just where we wanted to be: off the beaten path.

After several days of fabulous scenery and luscious food and wine, we headed toward the Alps in the Val d'Aosta region. Our first stop was Cogne, a slip of a skiing village, but there was no skiing because it was too early in the season, and there were no summer activities like hiking because it was too cold. In fact, there was absolutely nothing happening in Cogne. Every hotel was closed, every shop was shuttered, not even a restaurant was open. We wandered around the few streets, when suddenly with a start I spotted a huge poster attached to the door of a closed shop. It was a picture of the Twin Towers on fire.

And that was just the beginning of our trip where, from the top to the bottom of Italy, people hugged us, people cried for us, told us how sorry they were, how they loved America and all Americans. I had lived through many eras in Italy, starting in 1959, when my students in Bari heard I was from New York and asked if just possibly I might know their uncle in the Bronx, if I could explain baseball to them, and could I please tell them absolutely everything about America. Then in Rome in the late 60s and 70s during the civil-rights movement and the Vietnam War, everybody hated Americans because we were prejudiced against blacks, and told us to get out of Vietnam. I used to walk to work, and along the Roman streets would see graffiti everywhere that shouted, "Yankee Go Home" and "Fuck the U.S." And now, because of 9/11, the Italians could not give us enough love. It was bewildering but so satisfying to feel okay again about being an American. And even Franco was taken for an American—something about those button-down shirts or the shoes he wore.

Every night we counted out the pills, checking our little booklet: how many Prednisone for that day, when to start reducing the dose, how much Lasix to take. Not too much that we'd have to look for bathrooms all over the place, but enough so that Franco's legs wouldn't swell up again.

In Italy men like to pee outdoors with abandon, in the fields, against walls, behind trees, sometimes even in front of the trees. And not only in Italy. Before I went to live in Italy, I lived for two years in a small farm town in France. Each evening when the farmer came in from working the fields, he would approach his house, just next door to mine, walk resolutely up to the outer wall, open up his fly, and pee contentedly against the front wall of his own house. Then, after a few shakes, he'd zip back up, tug in his shirt, walk the few feet to the front door, and go inside. He had a perfectly fine, modern bathroom inside his house. But, somehow, you could tell from the beatific smile on his face as he watched his pee splashing against the wall, there was something so much more satisfying about performing this act outdoors rather than indoors.

As long as we were in the woods around his grandfather's house in Le Marche, Franco could pee outdoors to his heart's content. But in the cities we really needed to be more careful. Only once, on a day trip to Sorrento, we could not find a café or a restaurant in time, and looking around, what did I see but my husband peeing right there against a park wall in the center of the city of Sorrento. No one seemed to notice. I dashed into the nearest store and pretended to shop.

AS TIME WENT on during our saga of the kidney, Franco and I became more and more obsessed with urine, its amount, its smell, its color, its texture. How many grams came out? Was it foamy? How did it smell? Was it dark or light? Did it burn?

What about the Lasix? Should he take a bit more? A bit less? What about this other pill? More? Less?...

THE BOOK THAT was the basis for our trip did get published, but it isn't called *Travels with My Fork* with the subtitle *Italy Off the Eaten Path,* the ones we would have preferred.

It is *Italy, the Romagnoli Way: A Culinary Journey* and came out in 2008, happily while Franco was still alive to see it.

FRANCO'S FATHER

"THAT'S THE WAY to go," Franco said to me one day. "If I had a choice, that's the way I would want to go."

He was certain that his father, Luigi, had died in the very best way possible. One day when Luigi was 74, he walked home and entered the garden in front of his house in Rome. It was a beautiful day, so he sat down on the stone wall just to rest for a while. Franco's mother was in the kitchen cooking dinner, and as time went by, wondered why her husband hadn't come in yet. She sent one of her grandchildren outside and into the yard, to tell his grandfather that dinner was ready. But when the child arrived, he saw that his grandfather seemed to be sleeping, his head down on his chest. He pushed at his shoulder, and Franco's father slumped over. He was dead.

*   *   *

I DIDN'T CALL the priest to come. I knew absolutely that Franco didn't want a priest, lapsed Catholic that he was. He liked to tell me the story of his mother and father. His mother was very religious, regularly attending mass, and definitely wanting a traditional funeral service for herself and for her husband. His father was raised a Catholic, of course, like just about everyone in Italy, but had long ago become a non-believer. He told

41

Franco and Franco's brother that he did not want a priest or any kind of funeral mass; except, however, if they thought it would break their mother's heart—then go ahead and do it for her. But it would be for her, their mother, not for him.

Franco used to say to me, "When things get bad for us, let's just hold hands and jump off a cliff together." I said I might prefer pills. His next suggestion, and the one he stuck to, was that we would each pick up a heavy frying pan and hit each other over the head with great force. But then not too long after that, an article appeared in the paper that said: "Landlord survives alleged frying-pan attack." So that method didn't seem to have much chance of success.

I THINK A lot about what is the best way to go, because probably it will be my time next. There is no level above me, no parents or grandparents; everybody is now below me, children and grandchildren, so I must be the next. For Franco's father, it was lucky; he probably never even suffered for a second, a quick heart attack. But for all those who were left behind? They never got a chance to say good-bye, to give a last hug and kiss. Are we selfish to think that? Would we rather have our loved one get cancer and have a long and agonizing illness and death, just so we could be together more?

It has always seemed to me that what Franco and I had was something in between. Yes, he had been sick with kidney disease for a long time, but every time there was an emergency, another hospitalization, another scare, he would get better and always come home. So it seems we had the long illness but never the chance to say good-bye, because maybe he, too, kept thinking he'd come home again.

The husband of my friend Judy got up from bed one night and went downstairs to get a glass of water. Judy stirred at hearing him get up, and a second later, she heard a loud crash from the kitchen. She threw off the covers, raced down the stairs, and found him sprawled on the floor halfway between the kitchen and the dining room. He was dead.

I read Joan Didion's book, *The Year of Magical Thinking,* and thought, *What if I, like her husband, was sitting across from Franco at dinner, and suddenly he slumped over and was never revived?*

And then there is my friend who nursed her husband for seven years as his cancer grew so slowly and unendurably worse. Together they talked about his death often; they knew it was inevitable; they were preparing every step of the way: how he felt about continuing chemo or other medications, what kind of funeral service he wanted, did he want to be cremated, even what music there would be at the service.

I THINK ABOUT all these people and all the other people I know or know of who suffered one or the other of these ways for their loved one to go. And I realize I am in the middle somewhere, and is that because I was too ignorant to realize how sick Franco was ... no, of course I knew.... But then why weren't we preparing for anything? Somehow we both thought he'd make it, because he had made it so many other times. Whatever "make it" means. Nobody said to me, "Gwen, you are in denial," but now I am thinking maybe I was. How could anyone who had taken enough medical notes about her husband's condition over the years to fill two notebooks not realize that he was not going to outlast this illness? But then, how could we know that this was the time he wouldn't come home? Not a single medical person there in his hospital room that night ever said to me: "You know, this time maybe you should stay right here."

THE FAMILY DID have a funeral mass for Franco's father, but only for the sake of his mother. After all, would his father ever know? The mother would.

I knew that Franco did not want a religious service, so I never planned one. We had instead a lovely and inspiring memorial service where many friends got up to talk about Franco and what he meant to them. I think back to that day, and I think that Franco would have liked it, that it would have been what he wanted, a celebration of his life by people who loved him.

MEETING DR. GOGGINS

BIG NEWS IN THE BOSTON GLOBE TODAY, NOV. 4, 2011

New transplant center inaugurated at Brigham & Women's Hospital, donated by wealthy Boston couple, Elaine and Gerry Schuster. And there is a big photo of all the dignitaries spread out around the lobby of the Brigham. It says that Dr. Joseph Murray was there, now in his nineties, the surgeon who performed the first kidney transplant. I peer through the many faces in the crowd to see if I know anybody. I have spent months and months of my life in that hospital; I know every nook and cranny of the place; I know everybody who ever worked in the department of nephrology.

(Dr. Murray died in November 2012.)

*   *   *

WE WALK DOWN the long, long hallway of the Brigham and Women's Hospital until we find ourselves under the dome of the old original hospital, once called the Peter Bent Brigham. There the hallways narrow and darken, the rooms are tiny, there is dark wood paneling, no more of the steel and glass and marble that make up the new part. Even the signs on the doors of the offices are so small and dark, we have trouble finding the one that says "Kidney Transplant Office."

Once inside, we meet Gloria, the pleasant, smiling receptionist, her desk and shelves overflowing with the papers and books crammed into her tiny room. She tells us to wait in the next room and the doctor will be with us shortly. It, too, is small, with enough room for only seven chairs and a few magazines to read. As is my wont in the offices of doctors and dentists I have never met, I prowl around and peruse the certificates tacked on the walls. There are, as expected, the medical certificates of the two surgeons, but what first catches my eye is a framed copy of a newspaper article. It is from the *Boston Globe*, dated December 23, 1954, describing the very first kidney transplant performed with a living donor anywhere in the whole wide world, by Dr. Joseph Murray, right here at the old Peter Bent Brigham Hospital. It details the story of the identical twins, one of whom donated a kidney to his brother. The surgery was successful, and the man did not reject his new kidney. And the donor brother did well, too.

It was the logical organ to experiment on because we have two of them. We can give up one of them and continue on living just fine with the other one.

The accreditations of the two surgeons are of course prominently displayed—where they got their undergraduate degrees and their medical degrees, how many honors they have received from various medical and renal organizations. Dr. William Powelson appears to be the main guy, because there is a newspaper article about him, too. It turns out that he performed the first kidney transplant by means of laparoscopic surgery, that is, removing the living donor's kidney without breaking the ribs. From a look at his credentials, he also seems to be older and perhaps more experienced than a Dr. William Goggins. Every place Dr. Goggins went to school was in St. Louis. I wonder why. Is that a good medical school, I wonder? I've been in so many doctors' offices in Boston that all have those Harvard Medical School certificates on their walls, but never met anyone who went to medical school in St. Louis. Oh, well, we are waiting for Dr. Powelson anyway.

After about fifteen minutes, at the doorway appears a man in a white coat, so handsome—and so young—that he could be my son. In fact, he looks even younger than any of the sons Franco and I actually have. How can he possibly be that experienced?

He smiles an adorable smile and says, "I'm Dr. Goggins, nice to meet you." *Uh-oh,* I think, *he may be lovely, but he's clearly the second in command.* I can tell that Franco is surprised and chagrined, too, but of course we don't say anything and just follow him into another tiny, inner office.

"I have received the results of all your tests," he tells us, "and Mr. Romagnoli, you are a candidate for a kidney transplant."

We learn that if Franco could find a living donor, a willing family member who would be a "match," he could have a transplant right now. If, however, that would not work and he would have to have a "cadaveric" donor, that is, a kidney from a dead person, then he would not be permitted to get on the transplant list until he had first gone on dialysis. In order to prepare for such an eventuality, says Dr. Goggins, Franco should have a fistula operation soon.

"What is that?" we ask in unison.

Okay, this is what a fistula is.

The surgeon makes an incision in your lower arm, looks inside, and then ties together a vein and the artery that he finds there. He actually opens up each of them and makes them into one vessel. Then your arm will have this bump on it, and the bump will throb from all that blood flowing through it. For hemodialysis, a large, really large, needle that is attached to a machine has to be placed in your arm. All that bad blood that is in your system will come out through this huge needle and go though the machine to get purified, and then the new good, cleansed blood will be put back into your body. When you have this fistula bump, it is easy to place the needle in your arm. A nurse does not have to keep trying to find a vein big enough—it's right there, already made.

"But we thought Franco wasn't ready for dialysis yet." I'm sounding a little scared. "We were told his numbers were still all right." (Numbers continue to be everything ... you spend every single day looking at and counting numbers.)

"That's true," responded Dr. Goggins, "but let me tell you, the best fistula is an unused fistula."

"So why do it?"

"The fistula has to mature, it has to ripen, in order to be ready for the needle. If you make a fistula too late and have to go on dialysis quickly, it may not work. Then a surgeon will have to put a catheter in the patient's neck," he says, pointing to the space above his collarbone. "It would have to be done as an emergency procedure, first, and second, it is much more difficult for a patient to have to deal with tubes in his neck than in his arm. So that's why I would recommend scheduling surgery fairly soon. With good luck Franco may not need it for years, that's what we hope, but just in case ..."

And unused it would be ... for a year and a half, surprising all of Franco's doctors....

The day of the operation, I'm sitting on a bench in that long waiting room downstairs where the outpatient operations are performed. Dr. Goggins comes out, sits down next to me, and tells me everything that happened, how he tied the vein and artery together in Franco's left wrist. How it's going to be a really good, strong fistula, the arm already throbbing and pulsating with all that blood flowing through it. And then he waits patiently for every question I have, never in a hurry or brusque or matter-of-fact the way most surgeons are thought to be. They are so important, they are so busy, they give you the quick facts, usually not waiting to see if you understood them, and then they're off to their next important task. Not this guy; he acted as if he had nowhere else in the world to go, except to sit with me, reassure me, and answer clearly all my questions.

WHEN I THINK back to that day, and all the days that followed when we were dealing with kidney disease, I say to myself, *Thank God for Bill*

Goggins. I am so happy he is the one who came out of his office to greet us. Never once in all the time we knew him was he not personable, sympathetic, kind, and patient with all our questions—Franco would say *my* questions, and that would be true. Never rushing us, never showing that he had anything else in the world to do except stay and talk with us.

And then the phone call came.

"I just wanted to tell you my news. I am leaving the Brigham and going out to Indianapolis, where I will be the chief of the kidney-transplant department at the Indiana University Hospital. It is a wonderful transplant center and an opportunity for me that I just could not pass up. Here is my cell phone number; you can call me at any time."

Happy for him, we were heartbroken for ourselves.

GOING ON DIALYSIS

When I go to the office of my primary care doctor on the fifth floor of the medical office building, I have to pass by the office of Dr. Franklin Segall. As I walk down that long hallway full of offices, I am not always sure which is the door to his office, until I come up against his name, and I can feel my heart skip a beat, even now after all this time.

It was Dr. Segall who hooked Franco up to the hemodialysis machine for the very first time. Franco had begun to get weaker, until one day he said to me that he just couldn't live another day like this. He was ready. But I certainly wasn't; I had thought I could delay that dreaded day forever. I knew it would change our lives forever.

To me *dialysis* had been the scariest word of all the scary words we had heard—and were to hear—from all our doctors. And in the ensuing years, true to my fears, the procedure subsumed our lives.

Hemo—from the Greek, "blood." *Dialysis*—a system that would take out all of Franco's blood and run it through a complicated mechanism in order to remove his blood's impurities, and then put his blood back into him through that tube with its needle inserted into the back of his wrist. That would be the lump in Franco's arm that Bill Goggins had called an excellent fistula. Franco's kidneys were supposed to get all those impurities out by themselves, but they weren't doing that. So, I knew, I had to thank whatever person that was who had invented the dialysis machine.

Dr. Segall said that Franco had to be admitted into the hospital for the first two times he was on dialysis. Nurses needed to monitor how he reacted, to watch him round the clock, to detect whether any changes might need to be made in the workings of the machine.

I leaned on the wall in the corridor outside the dialysis room and sobbed. I cried each time I dropped Franco off at the dialysis clinic he was assigned to after those first two days, three times a week for five hours each time. Then I'd pick him up and take him home to sleep, as he was exhausted from the long and sometimes painful procedure. From that first day at the clinic, for us every week was composed of four days instead of seven, arriving every Tuesday and Thursday and Saturday at 11 a.m. and staying until all his blood had been cleaned out and put back in.

I STARTED SEARCHING for ways to get a kidney transplant. Dr. Goggins had already told us that to get on a kidney-transplant list you first had to go on dialysis if you were getting a cadaveric kidney. *Cadaveric,* an organ from a dead person, as opposed to a transplant from a willing and qualified donor. If a donor came forward who was a match, you could have that transplant anytime without ever having to go on dialysis. I was tested, but I was not a match. And so, in that spring of 2004, after he had endured an inordinate number of tests, blood drawings, questionnaires, procedures, and checks on family background, Franco's name was finally deemed acceptable to be put on the New England/Northeast transplant list.

Our search began, of course, with the Brigham. We went to see Dr. Powelson, who was extremely kind and helpful, giving us an abundance of information about how the organ bank UNOS (United Network for Organ Sharing) works, statistics about dialysis versus transplant, details on how long people usually have to wait, and many other facts not easy to remember. We left his office loaded down with pamphlets and articles.

Somewhere along the way, a friend said we should try the hospital in Providence, Rhode Island, because the wait might be shorter there. So we took one of those non-dialysis days and drove down for a daylong visit to the kidney-transplant surgeon there, again returning with a load of information. But not really feeling any closer to a transplant.

There was a five-year wait on the Northeast regular list for a transplant—the "regular" list being the one with the names of everybody waiting. A new concept called the expanded donor list had just been instituted, also known as "the senior list." Doctors don't like to transplant older people's kidneys into young people, because they would probably not give the recipient enough years, but they decided that older people could receive kidneys from other older people. The wait on that list was from two to three years.

Then came the call from that cell phone number in Indianapolis. It was Bill Goggins.

"I have an idea for you. I found out that you can sign up for the Midwest transplant list if you take your name off the Northeast list. The list out here is much shorter, so there's a much better chance you wouldn't have to wait so long here."

His "regular" list wait was only six months to one and a half years, and the extended, older people's list was even less, maybe only two months! The phone call came at the end of July 2004, and Bill had done forty-five transplants since January. "The Indiana University Hospital," he said proudly, "is the fourth-largest kidney-transplant center in the country."

Thus began a whole new set of evaluations. Bill urged us to come out to his hospital to visit and learn all about what we were getting into. And so we managed to steal two days in a row by changing from Tuesday to a Monday-morning dialysis, then flying out that evening to Indianapolis. We would stay Tuesday and Wednesday, and be back for Franco's regular dialysis date on Thursday. We had a lot to do on those two days: not only to meet with Bill, learn about the procedure, and meet the nurse coordinator who would organize everything, but to look around the city and find ourselves a place to stay for the month that we would be living there, should the date ever happen.

Everyone was really nice—that's what they say about people in the Midwest, and it's true—and we were happy to see Bill again. We thought about the luck we'd had that day when it was Bill Goggins who walked into that little waiting room and introduced himself to us. If we had never met him, we would never have known about the Midwest list. Now we might have a much better chance of finding that new kidney.

INDIANAPOLIS

TODAY I GO to the post office to buy stamps. With all the talk of the fiscal woes of the postal system, I'm always worried that the next time I go to my little local office, I will find it closed. Then I would miss the two guys I've been having conversations with regularly for years. But for today everything is okay; they are still at their appointed windows.

"Why don't you get the Forever stamps," suggests Jim. "They will still be good even when the rates go up."

"And when is that going to be?" I ask.

"They don't tell us anything, so we don't know, but we do know they will go up. So I have two kinds for you to choose from, the Liberty Bell, as usual, or the Indianapolis Speedway."

Just to hear the name of that city makes my heart go thump. I am not particularly enamored of fast racing cars, but I am eternally grateful to the Indiana University Medical Center, located in the heart of Indianapolis, for the kidney transplant that kept Franco alive for a few more years than he might have had.

The word, *Indianapolis,* conjures up so many scenes in my head, all of them as clear and fresh as if it had all just happened yesterday.

IT WAS 5 a.m. on the Saturday after Thanksgiving, the least likely day and time to travel on this major holiday weekend. A day one would expect the Boston airport to be in a kind of lull, awaiting the onslaught of passengers who would be descending on Logan the next day for their return home from family gatherings. And yet the Northwest Airlines waiting area was filled ... and so, it turned out, was our plane.

It just seemed to me that if you were going somewhere to visit your family, you would get out of town either on Wednesday or, at the latest, Thursday morning, and go back home Sunday, or to avoid traffic maybe Saturday afternoon. But 5 a.m. on Saturday?

They couldn't be going to a football game, because there wasn't one on that day. Maybe they were just getting away early from a boring time with relatives. I never did find out why so many people were going to Indianapolis at the crack of dawn that Saturday. I only knew why we were going—to get a new kidney for Franco.

*   *   *

EARLIER WE HAD been thinking: *What should we do at Thanksgiving?* All of Franco's kids and grandkids planned to convene at his son Marco's place in Vermont for the usual huge turkey dinner and all the trimmings, made by the many excellent cooks in the family. Plus, there would be snow and hiking in the woods, and sledding for the children.

The dialysis schedule of Tues-Thurs-Sat had been changed so the staff would not have to work on this major holiday. Franco's days that week became Mon-Wed-Sat, so we could have all day Thursday and all day Friday in Vermont. It was tempting, only a couple of hours' drive for us, but then, what if Dr. Goggins should call?

The cell phone wouldn't work up there in the Vermont hills. We went back and forth, trying to decide. We'd start with: "What are the odds that he's going to call now—it's too soon. We only got on the list two months ago; we were just in Indianapolis a few weeks ago for a visit. Things just don't happen that quickly in the transplant world, do they?" But then, we'd worry: "What if by some really outlandish chance, we should get a call and never receive it?"

I knew exactly what would happen: If we went to Vermont, we would definitely get a call and miss it. If we stayed, nobody would ever call. But what if? So the day before Thanksgiving, we went off to our local supermarket and bought two Cornish hens, some potatoes to mash, vegetables, and a mince pie. We'd have our own little celebration and try really hard to remember to keep the cell phone on, day and night.

It was the next day, Friday the 26th, about 3 p.m. when I first heard opera music coming from somewhere in the house. The drinking song from *La Traviata*. I knew I hadn't turned the radio on, but I could hear that music off in the distance. Franco and I looked at each other, and at exactly the same moment, we remembered the new cell phone. We had bought our very first one just weeks ago for the sole purpose of waiting for a call from Dr. Goggins. And then had immediately forgotten about it. Earlier, the two of us had spent hours trying to figure out how the thing worked. The phone offered lots of tunes to use, and I, an even bigger opera lover than Italian-born Franco, decided to pick a nice, loud, uplifting aria that we couldn't miss hearing. We called ourselves repeatedly from our home phone to the new cell number, just to be sure that it worked. Over and over, to the point where it had to be recharged, during which we would wait with bated breath.

When we finally realized what was happening, I raced up the stairs and searched for the phone. Luckily, it was where it was supposed to be, on the studio desk. It was Bill. Of course, it had to be Bill, because nobody else in the world even knew we had a cell phone. Then I thought, *Here we are, right at home; he could have called on the home phone number.* But would he have? A doctor so used to having to reach people on an emergency basis, he probably hadn't even written down our home number. But stop thinking about these things; it doesn't matter, because I actually got to the cell phone in time.

"Hello?" I said expectantly.

"Gwen, this is Bill. I am not sure, but I think I might just have the right kidney for Franco. There was an accident involving a thirty-five-year-old man on a motorcycle, and it sounds, from what they tell me, as if it could be a match. I can't tell you right now, because I am just now driving up to the hospital in the town where it happened to harvest the organs."

Harvest the organs, that's what they do.

"A thirty-five-year-old?" I asked. "How sad."

"Franco is next on the list, but if he turns out not to be a match, the kidney will go to the next person on the list who does match, and Franco will wait till the next kidney comes along. I will definitely call you back by six o'clock. By then, I will have the kidney and have done the testing. I can't promise anything sure, but get ready anyway, just in case."

I run downstairs, out of breath, and tell Franco. "What shall we do? Shall we pack? I bet if we pack, he'll call back and say it's not a match. But if we don't pack ..."

I can't help being superstitious and a major worrier about things that might happen but never do. And then I realize I hadn't given Bill our home number, because of course, we are not going anywhere this afternoon. What if the cell phone battery runs down?

Franco, being his usual reasonable self, says "What if we just half-pack; then it'll be fifty-fifty whether we get a kidney."

"What are we going to do for three hours? I'm afraid to put anything in a suitcase; I know it will bring bad luck."

We already knew from our visit in September that when the time came, we would stay in Indianapolis for a whole month. That meant a lot of clothes. *Well,* I thought to myself, *I could just start with the toothbrushes and underwear, something like that.*

Mostly what we did for three hours was pace up and down. It was hard to concentrate on reading a book. No one wanted to play cards. Shouldn't we be getting our things in order, I mean, like pay the bills? What about the mail? Who's going to take care of the mail? We had only moved into our new condo building about seven weeks earlier and hardly knew anybody at all. But then, what if we were still in the "big house?" Who would watch it for us? Keep the pipes from freezing? Shovel the snow? Thank goodness we had moved. All you have to do here is lock up and go out the door. No pipes will freeze; whatever snow piles up is someone else's problem; the car resides safely inside a garage, instead of out in the driveway day and night. So we are prepared, but never dreamed it could happen so soon after our move.

Oh, how the time dragged. We put on the early evening news. It was all about the crowds in the airport yesterday, how many flights had been delayed, how many bags had been lost, and then the usual homey scenes of large families around the dinner table with the giant turkey in the center. Oh, yes, don't forget the accidents. Busiest time on the road ever. Biggest travel holiday in the country. Lines of cars waiting at tollbooths. At least the weather was good: no snow; nice, clear skies.

Suddenly, the *Traviata* aria cuts through the sound of the television. This time the cell phone is sitting right on my lap. It is exactly six o'clock.

"It's a match!" says Bill excitedly. "I have gone online and looked for flights. The best is Northwest Airlines, leaving Boston tomorrow at 6 a.m., nonstop two hours to Indianapolis. I see that there are two seats left, so go immediately to your computer and book them. We have thirty-six hours for this kidney, starting now. I harvested it myself and brought it back here in my car. Call me back and let me know you've booked."

Darling Bill, he is not only a kidney-transplant surgeon but a travel agent as well. We are online immediately, find the Northwest flight and buy our seats for Saturday morning. Now, about the packing ...

We'll have to be at the airport at 5 a.m., so we make a taxi reservation for 4:30. If we get up at four, will we make it? It's midnight before we've finished packing, calling family, arranging for the mail, cancelling the newspaper. And then we can't sleep anyway. Franco is used to taking a lot of pills each day, but we don't have to take any medicines with us—they will have everything there, and besides, it will all be different. New pills, new regimen, new diet—no more dialysis! Oh, and today is Saturday, but we won't be going to the dialysis clinic. We'll be at the airport instead.

THE PLANE LEFT on time, the sky was clear, we didn't have turbulence, and we landed on time at the Indianapolis International Airport. Not two minutes had passed after we left our seats and walked into the terminal before our cell phone rang for the third time in its short life. It was a nurse calling from the emergency room of the Indiana University Medical Center.

"Have you landed? Where are you?"

"Yes, we've landed. We are in the terminal. We have only carry-on bags."

"Good. Take a taxi immediately to the Indiana University Medical Center. Tell the driver to drop you off at the emergency department. We are waiting for you."

It was about 9:30 in the morning and it didn't take any time at all to find a taxi. When we arrived at the emergency-room door, the moment we got out of the taxi, we were literally whisked inside by a waiting nurse and escorted down a long, long corridor marked "Emergency Way." At the end was a small room where we put down our two bags, took off our coats, and hung them up. I turned around and Franco was gone, having been immediately transported into an inner room that I was not allowed to enter. I sat in the outer room, chewing my fingers, scared to death. If I hadn't been so exhausted, I would have been pacing the floor.

Then our guardian angel appeared, Dr. Goggins, already dressed in his scrubs. He smiled that luminous smile of his and hugged me. There would be time, however, he said, because Franco still had to undergo more tests. Everything had to be checked out all over again—eyes, ears, nose, throat, heart, lungs, liver; then more blood drawings, EKGs, blood-pressure testing, all to be sure he was still in good enough health to withstand a transplant operation. "Meanwhile," said Dr. G., "come with me."

He led me through the hospital lobby, into an elevator, and up to the renal floor. We walked past patient rooms, then offices, and finally into a small room.

"This is the perfusion room, and there's the kidney," he said, beckoning me to come closer to a glass enclosure, within which lay an organ I could immediately identify as a kidney. It looked just like a drawing of a kidney in an anatomy book, or the lamb ones I used to see in the meat markets in Italy.

"This is the kidney that will be Franco's. There is no helmet law in Indiana for cyclists, and this state has zillions of motorcyclists roaring around every day. And every day there are fatal accidents. That's where we get most of our donated organs. It's very sad, but true. This man was only thirty-five years old and died wearing no helmet while riding his motorcycle on the highway."

"I don't know whether to be happy or sad. Did he have a wife? Children? Or just parents, maybe brothers and sisters?" I wondered aloud.

"We are not allowed to know anything personal about the organ donors. I don't know who actually gave the permission to donate. Later, if you want to, you can write a letter, send it to the nurse coordinator of our transplant team, and she will forward it to the family. If the family wants to respond, their letter will be forwarded on to you. But that's the most we can do about getting personal information."

I stood, transfixed, gazing at the glass case with its precious gift inside, feeling as if I were at Boston's Museum of Science viewing an artifact, like that brain they display, all black because it belonged to a fighter, next to the normal brain, all nice and pinkish-gray. The kidney was dark red and hooked to a machine that kept it alive. Dr. Goggins said a kidney could be kept for thirty-six hours before being transplanted. And this one had been in its case since last evening, when Bill had gone to fetch it and then phoned us. *So,* I figured, *this one will really be good, because now it has not even been twenty-four hours, let's see—start at 3 p.m. Friday, when Bill went to harvest it; call to us at 6 p.m., that's three hours. We left Boston around six in the morning, so that's twelve more, and now it's about noon, only about twenty-one hours all together. This,* I thought, *is going to go into my husband's body.*

Franco never saw the kidney that would become his. He was in the recesses of the hospital's basement undergoing all those tests, but Bill was still with me, so I knew they hadn't started the operation yet. I thought back to the time when I had worked at Children's Hospital in Boston and was invited by a surgeon I knew to watch a kidney-transplant operation. The scene has stayed in my mind as if it were today. On the table in one operating room was the mother, lying sideways, and in the next operating room was her teenage daughter, who would receive her mother's kidney. They sliced open a big gash along the mother's waistline and back (I couldn't watch that part) and then proceeded to break some of her ribs. Behind those bones lay the kidney. The surgeon snapped off a tube, then clamped something off, pulled out the kidney with his two hands, and placed it in a bed of ice in an enamel bowl that an assistant had brought to the operating table. Astonishing to me: an ordinary enamel bowl? It could have been in anyone's kitchen to use for baking. The surgical assistant then left the room, carried the bowl over to the next operating theater, and placed it by the side of the child's surgeon. The child's incision was on the lower side of her abdomen, on the right. The recipient gets the new organ in the front, and the real kidneys usually stay there in their original places. Since they are diseased, they slowly shrink and do not ever have any use again. Franco would end up with three kidneys, too. Except if he had had a live donor, the doctors would no longer have broken those ribs, because now they have a way of suctioning out the kidney. That was the procedure described in the newspaper article I had seen on the wall of the transplant office at the Brigham in Boston, a procedure much easier on the donor. Franco did not have a live donor, but this kidney looked quite healthy to me.

I began to pace and worry. What was happening? What were they doing to Franco? Bill led me gently back downstairs to the room we had first entered, but said I would not be able to see Franco for a long time. Then he disappeared, and I continued my pacing, all day long, walking around the entire hospital. It looked new, compared to the old Brigham, spacious, with wide aisles for walking and wheelchair pushing. Few people were around, unlike in the crowded narrow corridors back in Boston. It was Saturday, and a holiday weekend. Maybe Monday would be different.

It was now early afternoon. I went back downstairs to try to find those rooms again. A nurse was there.

"He will be going into the OR in about an hour," she said.

"You mean they haven't even started the operation yet?" I was really alarmed.

"Don't worry. Everything is totally under control. Don't forget, this is really major surgery, and prepping the patient takes a long time."

It was almost three o'clock when they took Franco into the operating room. The kidney had lived in Bill's car and then the perfusion room for twenty-four hours. Not yet thirty-six hours, still not too old.

*   *   *

I GO TO have some lunch in the cafeteria, and then wait, and keep waiting. My cell phone rings, now for the fourth time in its new life. It is Dr. G. telling me that everything had gone very, very well, not to worry, Franco is fine. He is now in the recovery room but not yet awake, and I will not be able to see him just yet.

I make my way slowly back to the bowels of the hospital's underground, down that long long hallway. Everything is dark. Not a soul is around. I finally find myself in that room the nurse first brought us to. Our suitcases and coats still wait. Down another corridor I hear some rustling, and discover there is the recovery room with the curtain pulled in front. I lift the fold and peer behind the drape to find Franco lying there full of tubes and IVs with one nurse tending to him. He is asleep.

"I'm sorry you won't be able to see him while he's in the recovery room. But after a few hours, he'll be transferred to the ICU and then you can."

The nurse is so nice and kind. Everybody in this place is so nice and kind. It makes me think of what my mother always kept saying to me: "The people in the Midwest are so nice. They are so much nicer than the people here on the East Coast, where everybody is rude and in a hurry." Mother grew up in Ohio in a small town, then moved to Philadelphia when she married my father. I used to get really tired of hearing about all those nice people in the Midwest, but now I'm thinking maybe her assessment of midwestern people was true after all.

Back upstairs in the lobby I wait, feeling relieved, but wishing I had brought a big long novel with me. Hours seem to pass before I am permitted to go upstairs and see him in the ICU. He is still full of tubes and IVs, of course, and still sedated, but there he is, alive and going to stay alive, they tell me.

"Go to the hotel and get some sleep. You'll be able to see him tomorrow in the light of day."

I hadn't even been there yet, but I knew that we were booked at University Place, the same hotel where we had stayed during our September visit. It is connected to the hospital by a most convenient overpass, and I stagger over it with the bags and finally check in. It is so late that all the restaurants are closed. The Sports Bar is the lone location still open, and I become its lone customer. "We're only serving salads at this hour," the barman tells me, so I order a Caesar and then as many glasses of pinot grigio as I think I can handle before I have to make my way up the elevator to my room. The barman and I become good friends, and I tell him I will probably be seeing him again for a lot of nights.

THE PHONE RANG at 8:30 a.m. I was petrified: *It's so early, what could have happened?*

"Where are you?" a familiar voice asked.

I hadn't even known that patients could make phone calls from the ICU.

"I'm on my way."

I picked up a muffin and coffee in the cafeteria and got myself up to the ICU floor. I was so excited to see Franco awake. Even though he was pretty groggy, his face lit up, and mine did, too. There he was, pale but content, with his three kidneys.

Our dear Bill had already been in to see him and said Franco had to stay in the ICU a while longer. He had had a little arrhythmia during the operation, a sort of racing of the heart, so he was connected to a heart monitor. He was also still connected to a lot of other things: a catheter, of course, and numerous IVs, one with morphine in it. The nurse told me that it was a patient-administered pain reliever, so whenever Franco felt pain, he could push a button and get some more morphine.

He was feeling pretty tired and mostly just wanted to sleep, so around noon I went down to the cafeteria and had my first real meal in Indiana. I chose the southern fried chicken with mashed potatoes and gravy, seeing as how we appeared to be in the South. I knew we were not in the South, but so many of the nurses and hospital staff had southern accents that it felt that way. Everybody calls you "Sweetie," too.

Toward late afternoon, Franco was moved to "the floor," i.e., the fourth floor, the renal-transplant unit. Our nurse was Sue Ann. Each nurse had a PCA, personal-care assistant, who was a nursing student. Franco didn't feel like eating anything; he was pretty uncomfortable, what with the catheter, bags dripping fluid into his arms, the blood-pressure machine constantly beeping, the morphine push, and the heart monitor.

"It'll all be worth it someday," I told him, and went back to the nice barman for a couple of pinot grigios.

IT WAS MONDAY morning, the first workday after the long holiday weekend, and even with the bustle of a weekday, the corridors of the Indiana University Medical Center were not so crowded and noisy as the ones we were used to back home. I took my usual muffin and coffee up to the renal floor and found Franco sitting in front of a tray of Jell-O, juice, and a Popsicle. But he still wouldn't eat anything. He said his mouth felt like cement.

We soon discovered, though, that the hospital has a catering service called Creative Cuisine. Of course, we hadn't tried hospital food yet, but with our (and everybody else's) experience that hospital food is notoriously lousy, we decided to try the alternative. Franco was only allowed to have liquids anyway, so it was hard to tell whether the half-cup of soup from Creative Cuisine was better than it would have been from anywhere else.

I spent the late-afternoon hours exploring the hospital lobby's various shops. I bought new pajamas for Franco at the gift shop. I peeked outside; it was rainy and gray.

On Tuesday our nurse was Kim and our PCA was Lisa. Bill Goggins came in every morning and told us how well Franco was doing. Then arrived various entourages: the chief nephrologist, with his retinue of residents and interns (this was, after all, a teaching hospital, which I took as a good sign). He explained everything about Franco's kidney condition. Next the cardiologist visited with his group. He told us that the heart monitor that was attached to Franco's chest by a lot of wires actually beeped over at the nearby Methodist Hospital. If the person monitoring the screen there saw something unusual or wrong, he'd call our nurse immediately. That seemed pretty weird to me, but then everything was so high-tech, and I am so extremely low-tech. The only thing I really cared about was when they told me that the heartbeat was just fine.

The blood-pressure person, the IV person, the blood-drawing person, the temperature-taking person, the oxygen-testing person, they all came all day long—and all night long, too.

Franco and I had taken to ordering lunch and dinner from Creative Cuisine, but since Franco still wouldn't eat anything, I ate all of his and mine, too. That took care of my visits to the Sports Bar at 10 p.m., but I missed my talks with the barman.

The catheter finally came out and Franco took his first short walk, unsteady and weak, but a walk nonetheless.

On Wednesday we had Kim and Lisa again, and we were getting pretty attached to them. Today was the nutritionist's day for a visit. A long one, it turned out. Lots of her advice was pretty much the same as it had been before we got the kidney: NO SALT. As for protein, it should not be a problem if the new kidney worked well. And how long would we have to wait before we knew whether it worked well? There was not a specific answer for that question, but I knew that was what she would say.

Franco could now walk to the bathroom and back, and even up and down the hallway for a few minutes, but he still felt weak and unsteady. Nevertheless, Bill came by to tell us Franco could be discharged later in the day; his heart rate was okay, and his blood pressure was slowly rising to normal.

We had our usual double lunch again, Franco still taking only liquids. Bill said we could go over to the hotel in the evening. To me Franco seemed too weak for that trip, short as it may have been, but Bill thought he'd probably sleep a lot better there. For five nights now, Franco had hardly slept at all, but then nobody ever sleeps in a hospital, with people coming in at all hours of the night and early morning to poke at you and take your blood.

We were given a red three-ring notebook called "Organ Transplant Unit: Discharge Education Manual for Patients and Families." This book contained all the information we would ever have to know about kidney transplants and their care. In it were pages called "My Daily Schedule," where we would write down every medication Franco took each day— and there would be many, we discovered. Then there was "Weekly Med Checklist," where you kept track of all those pills by the week. "Special Instructions" told you what each pill was going to do for you and all the side effects that might happen. Then came the pages all about vital signs, how you learned to take them by yourself, day by day, week by week, forever and ever. We would have our own blood-pressure machine, so that each morning and each evening we could take Franco's temperature, measure his pulse, and then take his blood pressure. There were so many pages for this section, I felt as if it would last longer than we would.

Our discharge coordinator was Doug. He came in about 3 p.m. and went through every line of the red book with us and explained how to fill out the forms, some of which had to be handed in at our clinic visits twice a week. We were not allowed to leave until we had taken the kidney-transplant quiz, all about meds, dangers to look for, the importance of hand-washing, watching out for signs of infection, care with lifting, and on and on. We both had to pass the test, and we only cheated a little bit, sometimes looking in the book for the answers.

We said good-bye to everyone around 6 p.m., when a nice, handsome basketball player came in with a wheelchair. Anyway, if he was not a basketball player, he should have been, being way, way over six feet. He would take us down the elevator, onto the walkway that connects the hospital and the University Hotel, and up to our room. There was the nice, comfy king-size bed I could finally share with Franco. He got out of the wheelchair by himself and snuggled into bed, looking really comfortable. Finally, he was willing to eat something: first meal post-transplant, spring rolls from room service. We scrutinized carefully our med schedule; up until now, his medications had all been given through an IV drip. Our schedule was 9 a.m. and 9 p.m., so at 9 p.m. Franco took his designated pills, the first of many that he would never be able to stop taking if he wanted to stay alive.

It was Wednesday, December 1, 2004, and from that day on, the red book became our Bible and never left our side.

And, lucky for us, Dr. Bill Goggins never really left our side either. A couple of years later, when I was worried about Franco and thought he might have taken a turn for the worse, I called Bill on his cell phone. He had always said, "Call me anytime of day or night, and I'll talk to you." It happened to be daytime, but on a Saturday, that I made that frantic call.

"Hi, Bill, I'm sorry to bother you. It sounds really noisy where you are."

"Yeah, well, I'm in Costco shopping with my kids."

"All of them?"

"Yes, but that's okay, tell me what's happening."

At that time Dr. Goggins' four children were under the age of ten, but he never hurried me, listened to my every scared comment, and patiently answered all my questions.

Dr. G., I love you.

BECOMING MIDWESTERNERS

THE MOST LASTING memory I have of the city of Indianapolis—other than its excellent kidney-transplant center—is its football team, the Colts. I must admit, I am not a football fan, though I hold a sort of preference for the New England Patriots because I live in Boston, and you can't live there without hearing about them all the time. It is also possible that before I went to Indianapolis, I had never even heard of the Colts. After just a few days there, however, it was impossible not to know all about them and their star quarterback, Peyton Manning. You can't forget a name like that.

The day after Franco moved into our hotel room, I made my first foray into the center of the city. Downtown Indianapolis looked like all the midwestern cities I'd ever visited: lots of tall office buildings, insurance companies, shopping malls, clothing stores, some hotels and restaurants, but nobody was living there. All the families, like the Gogginses, had gone out to the suburbs to raise their kids. So at night you don't find anybody walking along its streets: The city is dark and dead.

My mission that day was to find a rental car so we would be ready to move to our more permanent hotel room. Phyllis Martin, the team's wonderful nurse coordinator, drove me downtown to the Enterprise Rent-a-Car office. You really could call Phyllis "Sweetie." She was always there for us: driving me someplace, giving me directions to the nearest supermarket, doing all sorts of other helpful things that were way beyond the call of her real duty, which was organizing all the intricate procedures that are involved in getting kidneys for sick people. Phyllis told me that her job always became much more active during holiday times. Fourth of July or Labor Day—at those times there will be lots of accidents. And on top of that, since, as we had learned, Indiana does not have a helmet law, many of the donor organs come from people, mostly men, who die driving their motorcycles on the highways. Just like ours did. And Thanksgiving weekend to boot. At the Brigham they had told us that people at the top of the list for kidneys will actually check themselves into the hospital just before a holiday, waiting and hoping that a potential donor will soon be brought to the emergency room and prove to be a match for them. It all sounded so creepy to me, but having lived through it myself, I could understand them.

My next mission was to find some clothes that would fit Franco. It turns out that after a transplant, people hold a lot of fluid, mostly from all those IVs, so they get all bloated around their middle. That meant that Franco could no longer get his blue jeans to close around his waist. There is a giant shopping mall right in the center of Indianapolis, so extensive that I kept going around in circles trying to find a store that sold plain old pants. Nordstrom and other fancy shops seemed to dominate the mall, so I went back out on the street and found good old Old Navy and lots of sweatpants. I sit here today at my computer wearing those very same charcoal gray sweatpants that Franco wore every day that month.

My next stop was CVS, to buy a pair of manicure scissors to replace the ones that had been confiscated from my suitcase at Boston's Logan Airport. Then I found a Borders across the street and realized that we would need a lot of reading material. I bought *The Da Vinci Code* for Franco because it is very long and I thought it might be a good page-turner. (Instead, it was like reading a plodding tome.) Thank goodness I got a couple of Robert Parker mysteries, too.

When I returned to our hotel room, I found that Franco had slept all afternoon and might be ready for something to eat. All he wanted was ice cream. The food court at the hotel had closed, so I trudged back over to the hospital's cafeteria for some more of that southern fried chicken and mashed potatoes with gravy for me and ice cream for him. Franco was worried because he had hardly any voice and could only speak in whispers.

"Well, you are very weak," I told him. "What do you expect? You had a kidney transplant only three days ago."

Friday morning, December 3, was the day for our first checkup at the outpatient kidney surgical center. We had set the alarm for 7 a.m. for our 8:15 appointment, not knowing how long it would take us to get ready for Franco's first excursion out of his room. His new sweatpants looked great, and he could even walk to the wheelchair from the edge of the bed. We were making progress. I wheeled him back across the walkway and into the main hospital lobby.

The routine for the entire month we spent in Indiana was this: first stop, the surgical office, where we had to hand in our medication sheet, to show that we had abided by all the rules. A nurse then took vitals: blood pressure okay, no fever, weight still a bit too much. Then to the lab for blood drawing and pissing into a cup, and finally our visit with Dr. Goggins to find out all the results of the morning's tests.

I had gotten to pushing Franco's wheelchair around like a pro, back and forth to all these appointments, to the cafeteria for meals, to the gift shop, all the while swinging around corners with impunity. Both of us at the same time remembered Franco's famous words when we had met about whether I would be a suitable mate for him.

"I don't want someone too young, so that people will think I've gotten myself a trophy wife," Franco remarked back then, "but I need someone young enough to push my wheelchair."

That had been very funny seven years earlier when we first met. Little could we have imagined then that only a few years later, that joke would become a reality.

Bill's verdict that first day was that Franco was doing "as well as can be expected." Of course, I immediately took that as a comment to worry about—what do you mean, "as well as can be expected?"

"Well," he said calmly, by now getting used to dealing with my anxiety, "let's face it, not even a week has passed since Franco had major surgery; he has got somebody else's organ in him; he is seventy-eight years old. I think he is doing just right, considering all that. For one thing, look at these blood results. The creatinine is excellent, 1.6."

"1.6! That's fantastic." We hadn't seen a number like that for years.

"See? Okay, now here is your regimen. Take two Lasix a day to get the excess fluid off. I'd like to see you lose a kilo a day. Insulin ten NPH before breakfast, and ten before dinner. Same Lopressor dose for blood pressure. Prograf, very important, your principal anti-rejection drug; we're raising your dose from two pills in the morning to three, and up to two in the evening. The level to show that an anti-rejection medicine is working is the number 10."

I saw that numbers had come back into our lives with a vengeance.

We were cleared to move to our suite at the Marriott Residence, which would become our home for the next month. Franco waited in the lobby while I retrieved our snazzy, bright red Dodge Neon, already packed up for the trip. Our belongings now included our prized red three-ring notebook and a blood-pressure machine, on loan, so that we could take the BP twice a day all by ourselves. With help Franco managed to get into the passenger seat, and we were off for our half-mile trip to our new home.

Our room was not too far down the hallway from the lobby, and Franco did a yeoman's job of walking with only a little help from my arm. We entered a nicely furnished small living room, with a desk for our computer, a table and two chairs for our meals, a fully equipped kitchen, then a separate bedroom and bathroom. Our windows looked out on a lovely canal that runs right through the center of Indianapolis. They told me at the desk that the nearest supermarket was O'Malia, just a few blocks away, on New York Street. I stocked up on essentials: ice cream, bread, olive oil, juice, and pasta. With a few extras thrown in for me. Franco only wanted juice and ice cream again for dinner, but I decided to steam some Brussels sprouts for myself. I love Brussels sprouts and Franco hated them, so I figured this was my time to eat them. They smelled up the whole tiny place, so I never did that again.

The next day was Saturday, December 4, exactly one week from the morning at Logan Airport, and Franco felt well enough to get dressed and have his complimentary breakfast in the hotel's dining room. We made our way slowly down the hallway, only to find the lobby and dining room teeming with families. Tons of kids were running around; men and women were jostling for the pancake machine; there was hardly an empty table. What was going on? It didn't take long to find out. It was our introduction to the importance of the Indianapolis Colts and the fans of their opponent. The next day the Colts would play the Tennessee Titans, a team based in Nashville, a city within easy driving distance of Indianapolis.

For us, the much more important news was that Franco ate scrambled eggs, his first breakfast in a week except for the ice cream. After breakfast, I took another run to O'Malia, to buy our lunch but no more smelly vegetables. While Franco took his afternoon nap, I decided to explore. The weather had turned warm and sunny, so I took a long walk along the canal – it was lovely, full of joggers, people pushing baby strollers, lovers walking hand in hand. I thought, *I am really going to like this place.*

SUNDAY, DECEMBER 5, was another warm and sunny day. The same families were at breakfast, but this time they were all—from the oldest women to the littlest toddlers—decked out in Tennessee Titans shirts and hats. I detected just a couple of Colts shirts, lurking in a corner of the room. Later that morning, I set out for my walk into town, and after the first two blocks, I began to get the sensation that I was in the midst of a giant whirlpool. I was surrounded by hordes of people wearing Titans or Colts shirts, waving banners, carting coolers full of food and drink, singing loudly, a mad current of humanity moving toward the stadium which, I discovered, is right in the center of the city. And I was in the middle, swept along, but realizing that I was the only person in Indianapolis that day who was not going to the football game. I was heading for those downtown stores again, but I stayed with the crowd swarming toward the stadium for as long as I could so as not to feel left out, then turned left and headed back alone toward the mall.

The stores were deserted except for a few women here and there who hadn't gone to the game. I bought what are called "leisure pants" at Old Navy again, and the *New York Times* at the Smoke Shop.

Back home I found that Franco, of course, had chosen the Robert Parker book, so I might as well try to make my way through Dan Brown.

BILL GOGGINS WAS optimistic. Creatinine's usually scary number was staying low, at 1.4. That was always a good sign, not to mention that Franco had lost three kilos over the weekend, so the Lasix dosage could be reduced. But the anti-rejection pill, Prograf, had to increase, and a new one joined the pack: CellCept. And a urine situation had raised its ugly, foamy head. Why so much foam? Foam is supposed to decrease once a kidney is working properly; we all knew that. Bill surmised that the foam might have been coming from those two old kidneys still in there, unless the disease had spread from the old ones to the new.

"So fast?" I was alarmed.

"It is unlikely, especially with glomerular membranous. Never heard of that happening," he said, only somewhat reassuringly. "We'll do a twenty-four-hour urine anyway just in case."

WHEN WE WERE not in the hospital for an appointment, we read our books. But halfway through *The Da Vinci Code,* I gave up. I asked the desk clerk where I could find the public library, and he very kindly wrote me a letter saying I was a temporary resident of Indianapolis so that I could get a library card.

I loved the Indianapolis Public Library, an old stone building, perfect setting. I got my new library card from the very nice (everybody continued to be nice) librarian and pondered what it was I wanted to read. Something very long, something I would never have had the time to read at home, something classic, something I should have read years ago when I was in school but never had, something that it is imperative to read before one dies. Like Dante or Tolstoy or Dostoyevsky, or whatever the longest book is that Dickens ever wrote. I decided to start on *Anna Karenina*.

We followed a regular procedure now: I drove the bright red Dodge Neon up to the main door of the hospital, helped Franco from the car and into the lobby, where he got situated in a wheelchair. Back out to the car and the parking garage. Back into the lobby and we started our wheeling again, getting more proficient with each passing day.

As the days wore on and we continued our appointed rounds, we were encouraged that Franco was feeling much stronger and that the numbers seemed to be staying where they were supposed to be. Christmas was approaching and we were wondering if we would spend that day in our adopted hometown. We were thinking about getting in touch with friends, buying Christmas cards, not yet sure about our future.

THE NEWS TODAY: good old creatinine is cooperating by staying at 1.4. We deliver the 24-hour urine. A bit more adjusting of medications and Bill tells us everything is good enough to leave Indianapolis.

We make it home by Christmas.

I still have my Indianapolis Library card and the big plastic bag from the Indianapolis Speedway which we visited on our last day in the city and bought little toy cars for the grandkids. I am a bit hesitant to admit it, but I am always pleased when the Colts win – except maybe not when they play the Patriots.

THE RING

"When are you going to stop wearing your wedding ring?" a friend asked me the other day. "It's been a year and a half now, you know."

"Of course I know," I replied, "Why? Is there some etiquette book somewhere that tells a widow when she is supposed to take off her ring?"

When I was married the first time, at the age of 24, I was in Paris, my fiancé having been drafted into the army and stationed in France. We thought of ourselves as beatniks—as the nonconformist people of the 1950s were called—and would have nothing to do with convention, and that included traditional gold wedding bands. And so we found ourselves at a silversmith's shop on the Left Bank where the proprietor fashioned rings to our specifications. Each was a wide band with two silver strips that crossed and uncrossed over each other, symbolizing that we were together but each also stood on his or her own.

After he was discharged from the army, we moved to Italy, the country we had fallen in love with on our travels through Europe. There, especially in the southern part where we made our home, a wedding ring that was not yellow gold was not recognized as an indicator of marriage. So for years I was beset by scores of Italian men who were always following me—the tall, obviously foreign girl—down the street, teasing, nudging,

and making life difficult for me. Only after I got pregnant, and then began pushing a baby carriage around town, did they leave me alone.

Some years later and divorced (having become the uncrossed strip on
the silver ring), I returned to the States to live in Cambridge, Massachusetts. There I stayed a single mother for many years. When, at long last, I
met the new love of my life and we decided to get married, I told him that
I wanted a yellow gold ring. And it wasn't just because I knew we would
be visiting Italy often, Franco being originally from Rome.

"I want everyone to know I am married to you," I explained.

That was when we went to a jewelry store in downtown Boston and
looked at the array of gold under the glass counter. Franco knew that I
had never had an engagement ring, so without a word to me, he began
checking out the diamonds. I recognized instantly that the one he select-
ed was the one I would have chosen, too, though I hadn't even considered
it until then.

The wedding band that we both liked for me was eighteen-karat yellow gold, narrow, smooth, and simple, and just about as traditional as
you could get. The one we picked for him was also eighteen-karat and,
except that it was bigger, matched mine exactly.

Franco's illness later caused his fingers to swell. So, ten years after he
had put it on, he took off his wedding ring because it hurt his hand so
much.

"How can you do that?" I knew he had to, but it made me sad.

"I know I am married to you," he said.

Now that he is gone, I don't know what to do about my wedding ring.
I have been wearing both our wedding rings and my engagement ring for
almost two years. If at night I take them off, I can't bear to look down at
my naked left hand.

A friend of mine who was widowed told me that she took off her wedding ring the first month after her husband died.

"I didn't want to fool myself," she said.

Another friend who got married late in life never wore a wedding band at all, not while she was married or after her husband died. I have married friends who haven't worn their wedding rings in years.

I often find myself looking at people's fourth finger on their left hand, and I know a ring or its absence no longer signals if someone is single or married or divorced or widowed. Because now women do whatever they want about rings.

I had to wait sixty-three years for my yellow-gold ring, and I just don't seem to be able to give it up anytime soon.

BE PERKY

I CALL BETTY at ten-thirty in the morning, but she is out. I get her answering machine. I still have my nightgown on. How does she do that, I wonder? How does she get up, get dressed, have breakfast, and get out of the house? It certainly is not early, so it's completely logical that she should have gone out to do an errand, or buy groceries, or I don't know what. But then, she lost her husband more than ten years ago. I have been a widow for only two. So is that my excuse why I am so often unable to get out in the morning? Or sometimes even in the afternoon?

It should be easy. Just make myself go to the door, pick up the keys.

You have to go out the door. It's time to go out the door. All you have to do is just put the key in your hand, turn the lock, go out, lock the apartment door, and walk up the hallway to the front door. It's not that hard, so stop pacing back and forth across the living room floor as if you don't know where the front door is. Get the coat out of the closet, put it on, get the gloves, pick up the purse, you know where the keys are—in that bowl on the top of the desk in the front hall. You and Franco always tried hard to remember to keep the keys there, to be sure they didn't get lost or misplaced somewhere, as seemed to be happening quite frequently with various friends of ours. Just pick the keys up, just pick them up, goddam it, it can't be that difficult.

Of course it's not. So then why do I have so much trouble some days being able to perform these tiny little movements?

I finally manage to open the door, but then I will have to pass our building superintendent on the way, and, because he is such a nice person, he will say: "Hi, Gwen, how are you today?" And I will have to say, "Fine, Michael, and how are you?" What? Am I going to take up his precious time to tell him how I really am? Remember, Gwen, be perky, say "How are you" and then say, "Fine, thanks," though I realize that these days most people say, "I'm good." In fact, it might make more sense for me to say I'm good, just not fine.

Then here comes my neighbor Joe—he's nice, too. Always a smile to welcome me, and when I say, "How are you," he always says, "I'm terrific, thanks!" *How lucky*, I think. And then I wonder, is he really terrific, or is he unhappy inside, too, but says to himself, *Joe, be perky today. Be perky and no one will know the truth.*

Don't let on to anybody out there in the world what you really feel like. When they ask, "How are you?" don't say, "Shitty." That's okay with close friends, because they probably aren't going to ask you how you are anyway, because they already know. But now I have to go to the supermarket, I have to, because there isn't anybody else to do the shopping. I get myself steeled up for the person at the counter, so I can say in my perkiest manner, "You, too," when she says, "Have a nice day," or worse, "Have a *greeaaat* day."

Luckily, she stopped saying, "How are you?" a while ago, maybe because she thinks by now I'm fine, since two years have passed. And I wonder, when will the time come when I will be fine? How long does it take to become fine again? I think never. I cannot imagine ever changing from the way I am now. But people do; what about those people who get married again? Like Joyce Carol Oates, only about a year after losing her husband. How could she do that, I wonder? I am over two years now, and I can hardly look at another man who's around my age. And if I do look,

I see a stooped or decrepit, sad-looking specimen with barely enough strength to push a cart around the market.

But now I start to ramble. I am supposed to be thinking about being perky, so it will look to the world as if I am just fine. If only I could make myself believe it. And I will be fine, I know I will, sometime soon.

ADVICE GIVERS

"I CAN'T BELIEVE you've got that closet still full of his clothes. You should be giving them away by now."

"Don't make any decisions yet about your house. They say you should wait at least a year before deciding whether you want to stay in the same place or move."

"It's time to move on."

"How about going onto Match.com? There's also a Senior People Meet, too."

"Don't you think it's time to stop wearing your wedding ring? I have this old Emily Post book, and she says the correct etiquette is for a widow to wear her wedding ring until she dies or marries again. But you don't want to do that or you'll never meet anybody new. At least wear it on your right hand."

"Why don't you do some volunteer work or something? Get yourself out of the house. It'll make you feel better to do something useful."

"Or you could even go back to practicing law."

"Or get some other kind of job, if you don't want to go back to that."

"I wish you'd just try to relax more, take it easy, don't think about doing anything for a while."

"Maybe if you moved some of the furniture around or changed the pictures to different places, that would make you feel better."

"I think you should leave everything exactly the way it is. It's nice to have memories of him around."

"You know about that new research study—by the time six months have passed, you should be on your way to doing better, getting out, enjoying life."

"Why don't you go on a trip? That should do you some good, get out of here for a while."

"In my opinion the best thing you can do right now is just stay put until you get things figured out."

"Try to look at it this way: It was a gift! You might never have had him at all."

"I don't want to tell you what to do, but don't you think it's time to change your voice-mail message. How long can you keep saying, "Gwen and Franco aren't here right now?"

"I know that we never really see our own email addresses because they come on automatically, but did you know that yours still says "gwen-franco"? I mean, are you planning to keep it that way forever?"

"You're looking a little peaked. Why don't you go to a spa or something? At least go have a facial."

"Your face has a kind of flushed look. Have you been drinking too much?"

"What you need to do is have a couple of glasses of wine each evening. It will help you to relax."

"You should be working out more at the gym. Physical activity would be good for you, instead of just hanging around the house in your bathrobe."

"Don't worry about getting out and about, just take your time, do everything at your own pace."

"Look, I've got this book about bereavement and grief. I know there are a lot of them, but this one has got really good reviews."

"For heaven's sake, don't read any of those books about mourning and grief. They'll only make you feel worse."

"You really should stop listening to that Andrea Bocelli CD all the time with those romantic Italian songs. That isn't good for you."

"Remembering Franco is nice, but don't overdo it."

WHAT'S LEFT BEHIND

TODAY THE REFRIGERATOR broke down and most of its contents went bad. As I was taking everything out, I noticed the row of medicine bottles on the door shelf and picked them up for the first time in two years. There was Franco's insulin and a bottle of Epogen, the medicine that had given him enough strength to live as long as he did. I hadn't ever wanted to touch them; I had wanted to keep them there, to remind me of him.

Franco died two years ago, and this was not the first time I'd had mixed feelings about what to do with his things.

One of my widowed friends gave away her husband's clothes the very first month after he died. Her son took the ones that fit him, and she gave the others to a charity.

"How could you do that so soon?" I asked.

"I just didn't want to be reminded all the time; it was too heartbreaking," she replied.

Another friend, whose husband died a year before Franco did would visit, have tea, and console me. The third year after her husband died, she had finally given away his clothes.

"For me," she said, "they had become just things."

I know of a widower who kept his wife's clothes in her closet just as they were when she had died twenty years earlier, as if he had dedicated a museum to her.

Seeing Franco's clothes has given me solace; I couldn't bear the thought of looking at the empty space in our closet. For a long time after his death, I would open the closet each night before going to bed, gather up his shirts in my arms, hold them close, and be reminded of his smell.

When I first looked through his desk, I discovered all the writing he had been working on. I also found three pairs of glasses, his cell phone, his hearing aids, the walkie-talkie he had bought so we wouldn't have to shout to each other from downstairs and upstairs (it never worked), and myriad little quirky objects, such as glues and wire and a soldering iron, the things he used to make his sculptures. I put the glasses aside, planning to take them to the ophthalmologist so they could be recycled and given to the needy. But I couldn't do it, and I put them back in the drawer. I still needed to see them.

Then there were his shoes. For months and months I never touched them, feeling as Joan Didion had, after her husband died: *If he walks back in, he will need them.* Now that hope has dimmed. I finally took his moccasins out from under his desk, where they had resided for two years, never touched. I'll give the other shoes away (I can hear him saying: "Good riddance, I always hated those uncomfortable shoes") ... but never those moccasins.

What about that cologne called 4711, the one we had to special-order from that fancy store that sold imported perfume? Franco told me he bought it because it reminded him of his father. I used to tease him about buying cologne, but the bottle still remains on the bathroom shelf.

I'M READY NOW, ready for some things, anyway. I'll give the slacks to charity; they don't fit anyone in the family. I can no longer find his scent in his shirts. I will keep some, though, especially that old favorite one— the beige shirt that has two front pockets with flaps, the one frayed at the cuffs and coming apart at the collar. How many stores did we visit to try to find its duplicate? How many hours of our lives did we spend in futile attempts to find the same shirt? We never did, so the weather-beaten shirt with the holes at the elbows still hangs in the closet. I could never give it away.

I'll take the glasses next time I go to the eye doctor. It would be good if someone could use them. The ties can go (he never liked wearing ties anyway), but the ascots stay. They were his trademark; they made him look distinctive. I'll never give them up.

What about his Social Security card, his charge cards, his driver's license, those handkerchiefs with the R on them, and all those certificates and assorted souvenirs in the desk? Maybe next time.

ADMIT ONE

MY BOOK GROUP is coming for a meeting, so I take some of the coats out of the downstairs closet to make room for their coats. And there is Franco's beige windbreaker, dirty around the collar, stains down the front, coming apart at the seams. Of all his clothes, it may be the thing I remember him wearing the most. I reach into the pocket and I find a small piece of paper. It is a movie theater stub dated November 6, 2008, and it is for the Mike Leigh movie *Happy-Go-Lucky*, at the Kendall.

My son has written a book about Mike Leigh, the British filmmaker known mostly for so-called small movies, sort of slice-of-life films about the trials and tribulations of poor-to-middle-class families in London. In many of these movies, the characters speak in dialects like cockney or something else that is difficult to understand. For Franco, who grew up in Italy and for whom English was a second language, it was utterly impossible. But every time a new movie by Leigh came out, Franco would gamely say: "We have to go; Mike Leigh is one of the family," knowing full well that he wouldn't understand a word of it.

I look at that movie stub and the tears come again: it was the last movie we ever saw together. Later that month, he would go into the hospital, this time with heart failure. We had his last Thanksgiving in his hospital room, though we didn't know then that it was the last. After two weeks,

Franco came home again, albeit with a visiting nurse and home health aide for physical therapy to help him get better. Of course we would go to another movie together.

Then the illness that had weakened him over the years worsened, and by the second week of December he was back in the hospital again. He died three days later.

The day after I found that theater stub, Mike Leigh's newest movie, *Another Year,* came out, and of course I had to see it right away. It was the first time I'd been to a movie by myself in fifteen years. It was the show at senior-citizen time, four in the afternoon, the time Franco and I always used to go. We would sit in a row toward the back, looking out at all the twin sets of gray heads in front of us. And we'd laugh and wonder how it was possible that we had come to fit in with these people. Now in the row where I am sitting there is only one gray head, and it is mine.

As the movie progresses, I discover it is about an older married couple who live in London and often look back on their happy life together. And furthermore, the actors are speaking straightforward English, so Franco would have understood it. I think back to all the times I had to keep shushing him when he would whisper, much too loudly, "What'd they say?" And I realize how much I miss shushing him. Now I have nobody to shush. I think, *Oh, Franco, you would finally have understood a Mike Leigh movie. And you missed it.*

How does one get used to being a couple, and then suddenly, a non-couple? After my first marriage fell apart, I was a single mother for many, many years. During that time I went to tons of movies by myself and never had a second thought about it. It was a totally normal part of my life.

Not in my wildest dreams did I imagine that I would meet the new love of my life in my later years and then become so naturally and immediately one-half of a couple. But from the moment it happened, Franco and I were inseparable. We went everywhere and did everything together for twelve years.

He's been gone from my life for more than two years now, and I still cannot adjust to not being a couple anymore. How did I ever do it during those many years when I was single? And why can't I do that now?

I AM KEEPING the *Happy-Go-Lucky* movie stub from November 2008. It stays in the pocket of the windbreaker, which I hang back up in the closet.

THE WIDOW SIGN

I HAVE BEEN thinking about ordering a new sign: I will wear it on my back and it will say in big letters, "WIDOW, DO NOT DISTURB." That way maybe nobody will say to me, "Have a great day." Because I really can't have a great day, at least not yet.

Maybe then nobody will come up to me and say, "How are you DOING, you poor thing?" or "I am so sorry." And no one will send me a happy face on an email. Or say, "Have a good one."

If you ask me how I am doing, am I supposed to say, "Fine, and how are you?" or am I supposed to say exactly how I really feel? How do you think I am doing? How can I possibly be "doing" anything other than terribly?

I AM IN the health club, walking as fast as I can on the treadmill, and I look around at all the others on treadmills, rowing machines, bicycle machines, and all the rest, and I wonder, is anybody a widow? Are they all happily married? I look for rings on left-hand fingers, but I know wedding bands don't necessarily mean what they used to. Some women may be married for forty years and just not wear a ring anymore. Some men never did. Who are the single ones? Who is happy and who isn't? Who goes home from here to be welcomed by a spouse, and who goes home to an empty house like I do? A house where there used to be someone welcoming me.

It's just hard. One moment I will think I'm fine, and the next moment, something will remind me of him—like the ticket stub in his jacket pocket—and it starts all over again.

A widow who sent me a letter after reading one of my columns wrote: "I should have an 'Out of Order' sign on my back." She thought that if she wore the sign and dressed all in black, perhaps people would understand when she started to cry all of a sudden. And she wouldn't have to tell them how she was; they would just know.

I just got off the phone with the *New York Times* billing department, because I had questions about my bill. The woman I spoke to was very nice and polite and helpful, except that when we finished our conversation, she had to say, "And have a wonderful day."

I'd like to tell all these people who keep telling me to have a wonderful day, or a great day, or a REALLY great day, that they can beg me all they want to have that kind of day, but it is doubtful it is going to happen soon, no matter how many times they tell me to. But I know it isn't their fault. Their boss tells them to do that. Somebody tells everybody to do that: in the bank, in the shops, in the drugstore, after you talk to somebody at the doctor's office, or after you talk to just about anybody, even people you have never seen before in your whole life.

But then I remember the times when I have been shopping in the supermarket and out of the corner of my eye, I see someone I know at the end of the aisle. I am sure she sees me, but she ducks behind the shelves, hoping I did not spot her. She pretends she hasn't seen me. It is hard for her, too. She just doesn't know what to say to me.

So, I say to myself, *is that better for you? Would you rather have your friends and acquaintances turn away from you and pretend they don't know you?* Would I do that if her husband had died? Would I hide because I just did not know what words to say? Would I be too scared to confront the grief I'd see in her face? A condolence card, yes, but face to face, would it be too hard to look into her eyes?

And I tell myself to be more tolerant and understanding of the feelings of the other people in my life. What would I do if one of my friends lost her husband? Now I know what to say, but what if her husband had died before Franco did, and I hadn't experienced this grief yet? Would I have said, "How are you doing?"

I know it will get better, because time will pass, and one day I will truthfully be able to say, "I'm fine."

SINGLE SERVING

HE ALWAYS INSISTED he was not a chef, even though he had the first TV show on Italian food, had written many cookbooks, and had run three restaurants.

"I'm just a cook," he would say.

Whatever he called himself, I definitely preferred shopping at the supermarket together with him to going by myself, with the risk that I might bring home the wrong things.

"It's not artichoke season," Franco would say. "Artichoke season is in March. Just look at those things; we're not buying them. Overpriced, too."

He could tell just by looking at the artichokes that they were not going to taste good. "They will be tough," he'd say. "You'd have to cut away all those outer leaves and there will be nothing left."

Now in the market I look at the big, fat artichokes and wonder what he would say about them. They look good, but it isn't March. I pass them by. I'm not going to cook artichokes anyway if he isn't here to eat them with me. Then there are, once again, those Brussels sprouts, which he hated. Since he won't be around for dinner tonight, I could eat them, and he can't complain about the awful smell they make while cooking.

I arrive at the seafood counter and think about all the things I will never cook again because he isn't here to share them with me. Why would

I make that fabulous mussels recipe of his, then, when I eat them, just sit at the table and think of him all the time? All that trouble and Franco not here to eat with me?

I keep two place mats across from each other on the dining room table. That way I can pretend he is still here and we might even have a conversation. Not too long ago I saw that movie *The Young Victoria,* about the love affair between the queen and her Prince Albert. They had a happy twenty years together, and then Albert died of typhoid at the age of only 42. In his memory, each morning Queen Victoria laid out the clothes for Albert to wear, and she did that every single day until her death at the age of 81. There are times when I have forgotten to put out the second placement. But if Victoria could lay out those clothes for almost forty years, there is no reason why I can't keep out a second place mat.

The truth is that as Franco and I got older, we would often put the two place mats next to each other and sit side by side, savoring his spaghetti with Bolognese sauce while watching a movie on TV. And we'd laugh, remembering how neither of us had allowed our children to watch TV while having dinner. We vowed never to tell them, and we never did, so I can only hope none of them reads this story. Now, by myself, I almost always watch a movie, usually eating an already-prepared piece of chicken from the market, or just a salad. I don't feel like cooking anything, because there is no one here to eat with me.

Dear friends invite me out for dinner at the restaurant the four of us used to go to together. I try not to look at the empty chair next to mine. I gaze around the room and see that just about everybody else is a couple. When they are eating dinner at home, there are two of them and they talk to each other, or maybe they, too, watch a movie.

I was at the butcher counter in the supermarket the other day and asked the clerk if she would please cut one of the pieces of steak in half. She refused, saying it was store policy that every piece of meat must be purchased as displayed in the case. Clearly, everyone is expected to eat with someone else.

When Franco began to get sick, I felt it was necessary for us to be in contact with each other at all times. So, when I went to the supermarket, I'd call him and describe the fruit that was on display, or the zucchini in the bin, and ask if they might be acceptable for me to buy.

"It sounds as if they are too big," he'd reply. "Only buy the small ones."

"What about peaches? They're having a sale."

"I don't think so, I bet they aren't ripe." And they weren't.

When will I start to cook again, I ask myself?

I still remember well that cold winter evening when Franco appeared on my doorstep for the first date, that night I had the courage to cook for him. It was my spaghetti with zucchini and cream sauce, the recipe I learned in Italy, which I thought of as my signature dish. And now I am reminded once again of how he peered over my shoulder, inspecting every move I made. Then, instead of the expected critique of my cooking ability, I heard him say: "*Molto buono.*"

I miss him at the table.

THE NUMBER TWELVE—
AN ANNIVERSARY

I OFTEN THINK about the number twelve. Twelve is the number of years that Franco and I had together; the twelfth is the day of the month that we were married. If I think about the number twelve too long, though, I'll begin to feel sad again and I'll say to myself for the thousandth time: *It isn't fair! Why do so many couples get thirty-five years together, or sometimes even fifty, and I got only twelve? Why me?* As Franco said when he was first diagnosed with the kidney disease that eventually killed him: Why me?

When I lie in our bed at night, I reach my arm out to his side. I know I am not going to find him there, but I am reminded that he was once there next to me every night. At least for twelve years. But then, I think: *What must it be like for the woman whose husband slept next to her each night for fifty years? How will she ever get used to being alone in bed after all those years?*

I know that ruminating about fairness never helps. In the world there are assuredly many more who have had less fairness than I, and so I try to turn my thoughts to them. But before I know it, I am back to me. Why couldn't he have lived for more than 82 years? Look at all those obituaries in the newspaper where men are dying when they are 98 or 99 or even 86. Lots of people live till they are 90. What if he could have lived to be just 85? We would have had three more years together.

Recently I attended the eightieth birthday party of one of my best friends. The youngest person there was 73, and everyone seemed to be in good health. Franco should have been with me to celebrate.

Believe it or not, my father lived to be 101. I had just met Franco when my father was age 99, so I got to introduce my new seventy-year-old "boyfriend" to him. Franco accompanied me to the 100th-birthday party my sister and I gave for our father.

A good friend of mine who lost his wife a little more than a year ago is having a very hard time adjusting to life without the person he was married to for fifty years. He tells me that just three days ago was their anniversary, and he is going to call it their fifty-second, even though she is no longer with him. Why not? They had their fiftieth wedding anniversary together, so why not keep on having them?

This year September 12 would have been my fourteenth anniversary with Franco. Do I still have an anniversary? Am I supposed to celebrate? Do I want to celebrate? I haven't told anyone that today is my anniversary, so nobody will say happy anniversary to me, and that's a good thing. Because it isn't happy, except that now that it is the fourth since Franco has been gone, it isn't as painful as it was when September 12 arrived the last three times. Should I go to a movie and dinner the way we used to do? Should I go out with friends? Should I go to the same restaurant we used to go to every year?

Whenever we went out to dinner on our anniversary, Franco insisted on telling the waiter it was our anniversary. Then of course the poor soul would have to say, "Congratulations." Franco would then wait expectantly for the hoped-for follow-up question: "And how many years have you been married?" When we two gray-haired old fogeys said "Three," the waiter's jaw would drop, obviously expecting the answer to be forty or forty-five years. Franco took so much delight in showing us off as practically newlyweds and watching the waiter's double take.

I don't think that's so funny anymore. Why didn't we ever get a chance to say to some waiter somewhere, "Fifty years!"

Or, okay, even twenty.

A CHANGE OF SEASON

It is spring again, so I am preparing to do some of the yearly chores that Franco and I used to do together, like putting away heavy bathrobes, opening all the windows wide, getting out the sandals, and taking the down comforter out of the duvet. I have never been sure if you are supposed to say "duvet cover" or "duvet" by itself, but whatever it is, the change of seasons always brought the duvet task to Franco and me.

At the start of winter every year, trying to stuff that comforter into its cover was our most dreaded chore. We would stand on opposite sides of the bed and try over and over again to get the comforter into the right position so as to be fastened to the duvet by four clips. We'd inevitably end up screaming at each other:

"Hold your side up—it's falling on the floor!"

"It's too heavy; it keeps slipping out of my fingers!"

Then there were those stupid buttons that you had to button on the inside of the cover so they wouldn't show, even though nobody ever looked at that thing except us.

It is times like this that I miss Franco even more, especially the melting into hysterical laughter after the yelling had subsided. I recently watched a new documentary on Woody Allen, and they showed that clip from *Annie Hall* where the two of them are chasing the lobsters all over the floor. That's what it used to feel like when we had to shove the comforter inside that cover.

TODAY I WAS proud of myself: I filled up the container under the car's hood with windshield-wiper fluid. First, the challenge was to find that knob underneath the dashboard that would click open the hood of our VW Jetta. Then came the tricky part of getting my fingers under the narrow opening of the hood to locate the button that would release the hood all the way up. It used to take the two of us what seemed like hours to figure out where that button was. Even the Volkswagen mechanic told us he had trouble with it.

Then I heard a click and realized that, miraculously, I had found it almost instantaneously, a miracle, because I remember how much time Franco and I would spend swearing because we couldn't get the obstinate thing open. Now I just had to locate the lever that held up the hood, and then the hole it was supposed to go into. I looked down onto the array of boxes and wires and tried to figure out which one was the wiper-fluid box.

FRANCO WAS A master tinkerer, and his signature piece was what many called a Rube Goldberg invention. He had gathered up all sorts of pieces of metal and wire and tin from his basement work space and fashioned a six-foot-high fountain. It is a marvel of imagination and engineering, and everyone who has ever seen it was stupefied. Pieces of an old watering can, plastic cups, copper pipes, hoses and wires, tiny metal buckets, funnels, water and gas gauges, sink faucets, and various indeterminate objects had all been put together to form a perfectly working fountain. Children were transfixed as they watched the water spurt out from the top between tiny colorful flags, then travel all the way down through the various objects until reaching the bottom, when the water rushed up and spurted out once again.

It is a work of art. But it needs the yearly maintenance that Franco did every spring. I don't know how to do it, and nobody I know, however much they may understand engineering, knows how either.

I brought the much-admired piece into the living room for the winter. It may never work again, but I can look at it every day and remember the delight that registered on the face of every person who ever saw it.

TINKERING

TODAY THE MAN from the glass company has come, because the sliding doors and screens that open from the living room onto the terrace need to be repaired or replaced. As he opens the screen, it immediately falls right off onto the pavement, as it has been doing for months every time I open it. Clearly, he is going to tell me that a replacement is needed. He picks up the screen, examines it, and then carefully places it back on its track.

"What's that little metal thing down there at the bottom?" he asks.

I look down to where he is pointing: "Oh, that thing. My husband, Franco, attached that piece so we could use it as a foot opener. You know, suppose your hands are full of plates and food you are bringing outside onto the patio to eat; you just press your foot against that metal piece and the screen will open," I explain.

"Ingenious," he remarks.

"Oh, that's nothing. Let me show you another of his other inventions, as long as you're here."

And I direct him to the kitchen, where a toilet-paper holder has been affixed to the wall next to the refrigerator so that when the door swings open, it will not hit the wall. Instead, the fridge door will quietly nudge against the piece of foam rubber that Franco attached to the edge of the toilet-paper holder. When hit, the holder gently moves back and forth— just as it would do if it were in its proper place in the bathroom and you were changing a roll of toilet paper. Thus, no mark or dent is ever left on the wall. And this version is encased in a painted container, so, at first glance, you wouldn't know what the true purpose of this gadget really is. Or ever was.

THE LAMP

THE LAMP, ONE of several that Franco constructed, is sitting in the back of the closet in two parts. He built this lamp to illuminate his book as he sat reading in his favorite leather easy chair with matching footrest. To the adjacent table he attached an iron box, from which emerged a long metal rod that arched over his chair. The light from the bulb affixed to the end of that shaft would hit precisely the pages Franco was reading.

Now I find that the long stem has become detached from the heavy iron holder, myriad wires coming out of it and into it, most held together with Scotch tape. Would I have any idea how to use this again? I can't even figure out how to plug it in. The difficult question for me is whether I could possibly have the heart to throw away this intricate invention; but if I don't, it will reside forever, in innumerable parts, in the back of the closet, for my son to find someday when I am gone. And he is surely not going to keep a lamp that is broken and doesn't work, is he? And he'd certainly never figure out how to fix it or make use of it. It is also highly unlikely that Sean will just gather up the pieces of this lamp and keep them in the back of *his* closet. There isn't a millimeter of space, not with all his kids' stuff in there. So then he gets to throw it away.

As the years pass by, this dilemma is often on my mind when I see one of those wonders that Franco put together himself. What will happen to all these mementos, these reminders of our life together that I don't have the courage to throw away?

THE HOOK

THEN THERE'S THE hook he constructed for the bathroom door that refused to stay open and would always shut itself. It turned out that the whole door frame was tilted, probably a defect of the construction of the building, so there was going to be no way that it could be fixed properly without just about tearing apart the whole room. Carpenters came and went and all told us the same thing: it wasn't worth it. So one day what did I see but Franco lying on the bathroom floor just inside the door, hammer and pliers and assorted screwdrivers strewn around him.

"What are you doing?" I asked, knowing full well that he was up to another one of his quirky creations.

"I am going to make this door stay open whether it likes it or not," was the reply.

I didn't usually hang around and watch while Franco was creating his weird inventions; they were too intricate to understand and took much too long to wait out. When he had finished, I went upstairs to inspect the newest gadget in our house. I found that a metal ball had been affixed to the wall molding at the spot the door would hit when opened. On the back of the door frame, near the bottom, there was that short flexible stem that is found on almost all doors to keep them from banging against the wall. On the end of that stem, Franco had appended a vise-like piece of thin metal, like a three-quarter circle. So now when the door is opened and pushed all the way back to the wall, the new little gadget, like a vise, grabs onto the metal ball, keeping the door firmly in place.

A few months ago I decided to have the bathroom re-tiled because the paint on the old tile was peeling off and looking really chintzy. When George, my nice tile guy, had finished, I noticed that when he had replaced the molding, he had had to remove the metal ball. The bathroom looks fabulous, but once again the door refuses to stay open. Should I try Scotch tape or masking tape? That's about all I am capable of and I wonder what Franco would do.

I find myself so often wondering what Franco would do.

THE ORANGE BALL

THE TENNIS BALL painted bright orange sits atop the car's radio antenna, placed there by Franco when we first bought that car. This was an important appendage to our VW Jetta, because both of us always had a hard time remembering where we had parked the car in a parking lot. This way, we could just look around until we saw the orange ball and find our way to the car. Every few months the color would dim, becoming a shadow of its former self, and Franco would take out a can of spray paint called "Krylon Fluorescent Yellow Orange," with its label depicting an orange police cone that says: "Brilliant optical effect." And indeed it does have one, when newly sprayed. As the years went on and more and more SUVs and minivans and other assorted monsters would park near us, we would have trouble finding our car and realized that we needed a much taller signal. Franco was at work on that when he became too sick and had to give it up.

Unfortunately, the VW Jetta got totaled when an SUV plowed into the back of it a while ago. Luckily, I salvaged the antenna with the orange ball just before the tow truck pulled away. No new car has an antenna that sticks up outside, so I cannot put the ball back on the car. I would never surrender it, though, so the orange ball now resides in my living room among the various eclectic components of the fountain. A rare conversation piece.

THE WIRE SCULPTURES

FRANCO WOULD SPEND hours fashioning the most finely designed sculptures you could imagine .. out of simple thin copper wire. One of my favorite recollections is watching him sitting so contentedly in the corner of the living room at the wooden desk he had made especially for working on this craft. In a matter of minutes he would have wound a length of wire around his fingers and already come up with the outline of a ballet dancer, or a violinist, or a circus performer, or an animal. Later he would amplify these designs, and with a series of convoluted twists of his hand and wrist, turn them into little tableaux. Out would come the ballet dancer holding a parasol above her head while balancing on a horse; and the waiter prancing across a platform while balancing a tray full of wine glasses; a trombonist, cellist and violinist playing a recital together; the knight and his lady on horseback in all their finery; the circus acrobats piled up on a unicycle; and even the figure of Caligula holding his horse on a rein, pleading with the Roman senate to make the horse a consul.

I sit in my living room now, surrounded by these stunning and intriguing objects and feel as if I am living in an art gallery.

THE WEDDING

HERE IT IS again: September 12, the date that has a way of coming around more rapidly the older I get. And once again, I celebrate my wedding anniversary all by myself.

Franco and I were married in 1998 in Santa Fe, and sometimes I look back and ask myself, *Why did we get married in Santa Fe?*

Because this is the story of a bride who didn't know anybody at her wedding.

WE HAD DELIBERATED for many months about changing our status from "living in sin" to "married," with the final answer gradually becoming yes. But where and how? Franco's closest friend was a judge who presided in a federal court in Albuquerque and lived out in the desert just south of Santa Fe. Perhaps we could go out there, where it is breathtakingly beautiful, have the judge marry us, and then go on a scenic honeymoon trip around the Southwest. Then on our return, we'd have a big nuptial party for offspring, friends, and other relatives. Even though I did not know this friend, the idea became more and more enticing to me, and so we decided on this semi-elopement scheme.

When Franco telephoned his dear friend, Robert, the judge was overjoyed at the idea of marrying us. He and his wife, Jean, immediately started making plans to have the joyous occasion at their house. They would invite their best friends, and Jean, being an excellent cook (according to Franco), would make a sumptuous meal. So Franco and I started making our own plans: One thing for sure was that we would write our own wedding vows. So each of us set about putting our ideas on paper, then giving it to the other one to read. We were happy with our final draft.

Then the phone rang. It was Robert, with unfortunate news. He had earlier been a federal magistrate in Boston before transferring to New Mexico courts and had just found out that under New Mexico law, he was not permitted to perform marriage ceremonies. Only state court judges could perform wedding ceremonies out there, not federal ones, he said.

We were so disappointed. The whole Santa Fe plan had revolved around Franco's close friend being the one who married us. What were we to do?

On the next phone call, Robert said, "Not to worry, the wife of one of my colleagues is a state court judge and she'd be happy to marry you. Her name is Geraldine, and here is her phone number. She is awaiting your call so you can talk about what you want for the ceremony." Well, we already had our plane tickets; only a minor glitch. Our phone conversations with Geraldine gave us heart; we liked her immensely, at least by phone.

In the meantime Jean inquired as to the requirements for getting a marriage license under New Mexico law. As simple, it turned out, as any state's could be. Just bring your driver's license, prove you are over eighteen years old, and pay twenty-five dollars in cash. In fifteen to twenty minutes, you get your license. Then Jean went on to describe the magnificent repast she was going to prepare for us and asked us what kind of wedding cake we'd like. Phone calls were traded until a day before our departure—everything was in order.

We flew to Albuquerque, rented a car, then stopped at the administration building in Santa Fe and were amazed to discover that indeed, our marriage license took only fifteen minutes to obtain. Both of us being used to the frustration that is the Italian bureaucracy, we still find it astounding that procedures work so efficiently in the USA. Having time on our hands, we explored the Georgia O'Keeffe Museum and galleries of Santa Fe. Then, having been mistakenly informed that there were no florists in Santa Fe, we headed for the supermarket, where we bought so many bouquets of gladiolas that it looked as if we were headed for the cemetery.

We drove up to Galisteo, where for the first time I met the two people who would be the witnesses at my wedding. Their splendid house looked out on the desert and mountains in the distance. Inside, one huge space with a cathedral ceiling laced by huge logs contained the living room and dining room, with its long, heavy European table. The large kitchen was just around the corner of the L-shaped room. Sunlight streamed in from the myriad windows. I definitely approved of the location for my wedding.

THE WEDDING WAS scheduled for 6 p.m. on Saturday the 12th of September. Jean then informed us that she had invited to the ceremony and dinner a number of their friends, not a single one of whom was known to the bride or groom. "Oh, but you'll like them a lot," she reassured us. "There will be five judges in attendance." This news prompted me to begin thinking of this event as more of a trial than a wedding. I became apprehensive: There I was, far from home, knowing no one.

The morning of the wedding was filled with activity. The groom, who, besides being a chef and author, was an excellent photographer, sculptor, and tinkerer, and so was set to the task of repairing an intricate iron lamp that was broken. Jean began cutting up chickens and otherwise preparing the food. Robert was moving from room to room attempting to catch the field mice, and the bride was ironing her skirt and jacket and the bridegroom's suit. Everyone participated in arranging the gladiolas around the room. Then the gorgeous long table was set for ten with a brand new tablecloth and napkins, assorted china, silver, and crystal. At two the bridegroom took his customary nap.

Later in the afternoon the house filled with the fabulous smells of tortelloni with cream sauce and baked chicken. Then it was time for everyone to get dressed. Starting around five-thirty the guests became to arrive. First, the state court judge, Geraldine Rivera, our officiator, with her husband, Bill Deaton, a federal magistrate. A few minutes later, Ruth and Paul Kelly came in, he not just any old judge, but one belonging to the Tenth Circuit Court of Appeals. The bride, a lawyer, was left agape at that introduction. And, finally, there appeared Mary and Bruce Black, he another federal court judge. All apprehension at the overload of judges disappeared immediately, however. Everyone was totally down to earth, warm, and friendly. In five minutes we felt as if we'd known everybody forever.

GERALDINE WAS COMPLETELY up-to-date on instructions for the ceremony, so it took only a couple of minutes to review some details with her. Then we sought out a photographer, asking each guest about his or her experience taking pictures. Strangely, no one owned up to knowing how to use a camera until Bill Deaton volunteered, saying he'd once been a sort of photographer. We gave him our fancy Nikon and asked Bruce the novice to try the little point-and-shoot. We arranged ourselves in one corner of the room, Jean at my side and Robert at Franco's side. The ceremony was very short, probably a maximum of three minutes, with Franco constantly perturbed that Bill was holding his finger over the lens. Finally, halfway into the ceremony, he decided to stop gesturing frantically and left our little group to show Bill what he should be doing with that Nikon. It made a difference—you can't see any of the people on the first half of the roll because of Bill's finger, as well as the sun's being directly in the lens. The pictures on the second half of the roll are fine. Franco did not, however, miss a beat, and managed to say his part of the ceremony flawlessly.

The champagne began to flow just as soon as Geraldine had finished saying, "By the power vested in me..." A gorgeous array of hors d'oeuvres appeared on the scene, and many glasses of bubbly were consumed. It was as if Franco and I ourselves had invited these dear old friends to our wedding! The dinner lasted for hours as Jean brought course after course to the table. Finally, the chocolate mousse cake arrived, as dense and rich as possible. Because we had no little bride and groom to place on it, we took down from the mantelpiece the wire sculpture that Franco had once given to Robert and Jean, and set it on top.

Two of the guests even brought presents, a Nambe vase and a Santa Fe cookbook. So there you have a wedding where the guests did not know the bride and groom, and the bride knew nobody except, luckily, the groom.

*   *   *

TONIGHT, AS I write, it is the tenth anniversary of 9/11, and we are all feeling once again the extreme sadness of that day. When our anniversary in 2001 came, we said to each other, *Aren't we glad we didn't get married on September 11th instead of the 12th? It would feel so strange to celebrate.* Now it seems strange to celebrate our anniversary at any time, but I will recall that day in 1998 in Santa Fe and wonder what all those guests of mine are doing—the guests that I have never seen again since my wedding day.

HEARING HIS VOICE

I AM WALKING in Filippello Park in Watertown, where Franco and I used to take walks together. Suddenly I hear a voice saying: "Why do you take such short strides when you walk? You're tall and you have long legs; you should take long steps."

I hear Franco's voice so often, it's as if it were just yesterday.

The problem is that my physical therapist told me I should be taking shorter strides, because long ones are not good for someone with a bad back. So I have this dilemma; whom to listen to?

People often say to me: "Franco is looking down at you." I look up at the sky and wonder if that could be so. And if he is, does he still disapprove of the short steps?

BACK HOME I am doing the laundry, and suddenly I hear the washing machine creaking along its spin cycle but not actually spinning. I know, I put too many towels in it again, and they are going to come out soaking wet.

"See? I told you, if you put only towels in the machine, the load is too heavy, so the spinner won't work properly. You'll see, they'll come out all wet."

And they did. Why can't I remember that about the towels? We even once saw a movie where the wife put only towels in the washing machine, and her husband reprimanded her because they came out wet. I couldn't believe there was actually a scene like that in a movie, and I can almost still feel the black-and-blue marks on my arm from Franco poking at me.

I DECIDE TO have pasta for dinner and start to boil the water.

"Don't put the salt in the water now. It won't do any good. You have to wait for the water to boil and then put in the salt."

I am about to turn off the light and go upstairs to bed, but I notice I've left unwashed dishes in the sink.

"Never leave dirty dishes in the sink overnight; you'll regret it in the morning when you get up and have to look at them."

We never used the dishwasher for the two of us, and I certainly don't use it now just for one. Well, he isn't here, so I can just leave the dishes right where they are, or I can go upstairs and feel bad, knowing I will hate to see them still waiting for me in the morning. So I'm back at the sink washing the dishes.

I'VE FINISHED LEAFING through one of those ubiquitous women's fashion magazines that keep coming in the mail, and I'm heading toward my computer.

"Are you really going to order something from a catalog again? You know you're only going to end up sending it back."

It's true. I usually did return things and then get mad at myself for all the hassle that would entail. I pause.

IS IT POSSIBLE that you can live—are living—without the person you love, and yet that person keeps showing up?

I have finished peeling celery stalks and cutting them up to make chicken salad. As I begin to scoop up the celery strings in the sink to throw them in the garbage can, someone again is talking to me.

"You should put that stuff down the disposal, you know."

The plumber always told me not to put celery strings or onion skins and things like that down the disposal because they would clog it up.

"Nonsense," I hear him say. "I've put celery strings down the disposal all my life—I mean, for as long as I had a disposal—and nothing ever happened."

If he were here, Franco would have already swept up those celery strings right into the disposal and turned it on. I know that he considered himself to be practically a master plumber, but I am not ready to try the disposal, especially with him not here to fix it when it stops working. So I carefully collect the strings and put them in the trash bin, but wishing he were here to contradict me.

It was much more fun then.

FILIPPELLO PARK

THE SAME TREE that always started changing its colors to red in late August is changing its colors now; the same cloud formations that Franco loved to look at are up in the bright blue sky right now; the screams from the toddlers running through the water park are the same screams that used to come from our two-year-old grandson.

I walk around the path of Filippello Park as often as I can, and as I walk, I do my neck exercises. Turn to the left, to the right, look down, look up. As I look up I see again that pristine blue sky with those puffy white clouds, the same ones Franco and I looked at when we walked together in this park.

He adored anything that was in the sky: clouds, birds, airplanes, gliders; he had once flown gliders all by himself. Few people were aware that he had gotten his degree at Rome University in aeronautical engineering. He knew all about clouds and could identify for me: cumulus, nimbus, cirrus, stratus, and which of them would portend good weather and which one a storm coming. Then he'd ask if I could see the unicorn in that formation. When we were in Ushuaia, at the very bottom tip of Argentina, he could even tell me the names of all the constellations in the Southern Hemisphere.

Now in my third August walking around the park alone, I still look up.

If he were looking down at me from anywhere, it would have to be from those clouds.

These are the very best days. The late August days in New England, when it is still warm but there is a hint of fall in the air. Franco always said, "After Ferragosto (the major Italian holiday on August 15), summer starts to fade away and you can feel that fall is coming." He was right again this year.

These are the days when you can take long walks and feel the hot sun, but not get steamy and sweaty; you can feel the soft breezes on the sleeves of your shirt, and never want to go back inside.

The skinny little boys, so much like another grandson, Rory, are running through the water park, arms and legs all akimbo or askew or awry. I love those three words. Especially *awry,* which always reminds me of Sean when he was young. He was reading a book to me one day and said, "Things went awe-ree!" Actually, if you look at that word, that is exactly how it should be pronounced, and from then on, I have never been able to pronounce it correctly. It will always be *awe-ree* to me.

Walking in this place brings back to me all kinds of memories. When Franco and I were in the park, we would often look back on the days when our children were little, and marvel at a new phenomenon: fathers.

When we'd arrive at the park, we knew exactly what we'd see when the minivans pulled up. The fathers would get out and unbuckle the children from their car seats. One by one they'd lift them to the sidewalk, go around to the back of the van, and extract tricycles, scooters, bicycles, sacks full of helmets and kneepads, soccer balls, baseballs, baseball bats. This has become my favorite sight here: the fathers alone with their kids— strapping on the helmets and the knee pads for a scooter ride; teaching them to play baseball; holding onto strollers while they jog around the path; opening up picnic baskets on the lawn; changing diapers on the benches; pushing the child on the swing, where she shouts in unison with all the others: "Again, again!" There is hardly a mother in sight.

When Franco and I were young, we never saw a father alone with his children in any park or field or jungle gym. Not here in the U.S., and certainly not in Italy. When my son was little, we would go on weekend afternoons to one or another of Rome's glorious parks. There he would play with the other children while I sat on a bench watching with all the other mothers, the nannies, the maids, the foreign au pair girls, but nary a man. It is of great importance to make a *bella figura* (that is, to always make a good public appearance) in Italy, so children were always dressed in their best clothes to go to the park. That would cause the perpetual refrain to be heard: "*Non ti sporcare!*" "Don't get dirty!" Every time children got too far into the sandbox or into the dirt under the swing, their mothers would make them come out immediately so they could stay clean.

Now I watch kids with raggedy T-shirts and jeans with holes in them, running and skidding in the dirt, racing after Frisbees, jumping off the slide into the sand, or rolling all over the grass with their dogs. They are having a ball, and after all, there's a washing machine at home.

As I circle the path, I am listening once again to the Rach 3 on the iPod Sean gave me for Christmas last year. Obviously a big favorite of mine, Rachmaninoff somehow makes Filippello Park feel majestic, though that is probably not an adjective anybody else would use. This is, after all, just your plain old city park. On Saturday and Sunday afternoons its two fields are filled with children and teenagers playing soccer, and generally not a word of English can be heard. The teams are a wonderful international mix of Armenians, Indians, and Hispanics.

The walking path, on the other hand, is for everyone: those fathers holding the bikes of the kids they are teaching to ride, the teenagers on scooters, the middle-aged joggers, and others like us, older people just out for a stroll. In fact, today I see again that couple I often see here: "elderly" is probably what people would call them, and they could be us. They are walking arm in arm ever so slowly around the track. When we started our walks on that track around the park, Franco was faster, and I had a hard time keeping up with him. But as the years went on and he got sicker, I'd be faster, and he would lag behind. Or he'd be just like that husband I see today, sitting down on the nearest bench, resting.

CEMETERIES

It was dawn when I walked down the flight of slippery steps to the embankment of the Tiber River, clutching the plastic bag. Sean was with me. We continued along the edge of the jetty, looking for a quiet spot. We were near Ponte Garibaldi, where the water begins to roil and bubble, coming in waves like a miniature waterfall. We stopped when we saw a large, smooth stone jutting out over the water, then made our way onto the stone. I opened the plastic bag I was carrying, and we watched Franco's ashes flow down the river.

I had had to take these ashes out of the box that has been in my closet since the day it was handed to me. It was the first time I had ever opened it, the first time I had ever seen what ashes looked like. It took me a moment, but I managed to scoop some out, put them in the plastic container, and pack them into my suitcase.

He had never said what he wanted, so I was the one who decided to take his ashes to Rome, his beloved hometown, and the city I had lived in for so many years. I think he would have approved.

Back home, in the Boston area, I live between two cemeteries. When Franco and I first moved to this condo, people said, "Oh, I know that building. It's between two cemeteries. Should be very quiet."

As I write at my computer, I can look out the window at Mount Auburn Cemetery, the beautifully landscaped graveyard of Cambridge, Massachusetts. It is a magnificent place, with its exotic flora, brilliant fall foliage, blossoming trees in the spring. Among its paths and flowers, its monuments and its lakes, are buried an eclectic mix of famous people: Henry Wadsworth Longfellow, Bernard Malamud, Fannie Farmer, Felix Frankfurter, Charles Bulfinch, Mary Baker Eddy, Oliver Wendell Holmes, Edwin Land of the Polaroid camera, Winslow Homer, and Henry Cabot Lodge. Its spectacular grounds are frequented in all seasons by birdwatchers, artists, photographers, and all manner of people taking leisurely strolls or power walks.

The Cambridge Cemetery, down the street, is plainer, simpler, but lovely. It is the place where flags and balloons were left on many graves when the Red Sox won the World Series in 2004. Notes said things like, "See, you just had to have faith!" and "I know you are looking down at this fabulous celebration!"

I remember those messages and wonder: *Is there anybody really looking down?*

Franco and I often took long walks together on the paths of Mount Auburn Cemetery, the very place where Franco's name is now engraved on a stone. It never seemed to be a place full of dead people. It was just one of our favorite places to take a walk. As he and I enjoyed the serenity of our walks, I would sometimes have the most disconcerting thoughts: *Can anyone below hear us walking? If Franco and I were one day under the ground here, would we be able to hear the footsteps of those walking above us?*

When we took our walks, I would say to him, "I want to be buried with you; I want us to be together."

Franco found it hard to answer. When his first wife died, he had bought two spaces on her stone. He would just say, "Don't worry, we'll be together."

So when I found myself at the cemetery to see the director about Franco's grave, I was the one left to make the decision.

"I understand," I said, "that his name should be engraved on the stone he already bought, so his children and grandchildren can come there. But maybe I could get a stone just for the two of us."

The man looked at me pensively, thought a moment, and finally said: "I don't think you can have his name on two stones, but you could engrave something like 'In memory of Franco' on your stone."

"Yes," I said, "maybe that's what I'll do."

I HARDLY EVER go to the cemetery. I don't know how people do that so often: putting flowers on the grave, changing the water in the vase, brushing the leaves off the stone, sitting there. I don't want to see his name on the gravestone. It makes me shudder just thinking about it.

I do still walk there sometimes, but I don't look at his name, knowing he isn't really there, anyway.

AS SEAN AND I walked back up the steps from the Tiber, I stopped and looked back at the river along which Franco and I had so often walked together.

Was he here? Was he in Cambridge? Maybe he is between the two, as I am, between two cemeteries.

A FULL-TIME JOB

THERE ARE TIMES when I wish I had my full-time job back. I knew exactly what to do each day: wake up and say good morning to Franco, get up and go around to his side of the bed to see how he was doing that day. Then I would put on my glasses so I could read the numbers on the big dialysis machine, which stood on the table next to Franco's side of the bed—the table he had made himself when we found out that, after weeks of training, we had passed the test for doing dialysis by ourselves at home. On a piece of paper I would write down the necessary numbers, to be later transcribed to our "kidney book," the ongoing saga of Franco's illness. Next I would put on the latex gloves, hand a surgical mask to Franco, put a mask on myself, and lift up the T-shirt he always wore to sleep in. With both of us sanitarily protected, I could detach the large tube that connected his belly to the machine, the machine through which his blood had passed all night long and become purified. A happy substitute for the days when Franco had gone to the clinic for dialysis three times a week. After I checked the contents of the big plastic bag to be sure the liquid inside was clear and not murky, a sure sign of infection, Franco could get up and start the day. So could I.

Unlike the previous part-time jobs, which consisted of dialysis in the clinic or weekly post-transplant visits or various hospitalizations lasting anywhere from two days to a week, this particular job was a daily one, and one that started all too soon after our celebratory time in Indianapolis.

On our return home from our adopted midwestern city, we were back at the Brigham and Women's Hospital to continue our constant monitoring of kidney number two, or number three, if you still count both old ones. This time we were given a big, black three-ring notebook, divided into the same old sections, keeping track of the same old numbers—with that pesky creatinine still our number-one concern. Regular visits to the hospital for checkups had to happen every week. By April it was clear that something was awry (that word again); creatinine had crept up to 2-something, and there was that foam in the urine again. We got in touch with Dr. Goggins, and he remembered that the foam had happened right after the transplant and he'd thought it could be the two old kidneys. Now he and our new doctors were thinking differently. Could the new kidney be sick already? Dr. G. said he had never had a case of recurring membranous, but Franco kept feeling weaker and extremely fatigued.

Nobody said, "It's like déjà vu all over again," but I couldn't help thinking that to myself and wondering if the doctors were thinking it, too. And so, exactly five months after the transplant, another biopsy was prescribed, this time of the new kidney. Much to our chagrin, it was announced that, indeed, this brand-new organ had gotten membranous. It was Franco's immune system itself that was doing this, and no doctor knew why. They tried to make us feel better by telling us this time was different, because it had been caught much earlier. And so a whole new regimen of drugs was prescribed, one that completely filled up the new black three-ring notebook. We were constantly on the phone with Dr. Goggins, who liked to remind us that Franco was "no spring chicken" but that this disease was treatable. "It is not a rejection," he said, as if that reassurance were helpful, "it is just simply membranous all over again." Franco was too old and his situation too risky for him to be a candidate for another transplant. And so we plodded on, filling up notebooks with numbers and trying all kinds of new medicines and theories, as the devil creatinine kept rising on us.

Our other favorite nephrologist, Dr. Kathryn Tinckam, took us on at the Brigham in the summer of 2005. She is young and beautiful and smart and Canadian, and she and I still exchange Christmas cards even now that she is back in Toronto and married with adorable twins. We saw her every Friday for the usual tests and together watched the creatinine inching its way up. Nevertheless, she allowed us to take the trip to Italy that we had planned. We went in September to explore even more carefully the Le Marche region, about which we hoped to write a book. We made it back safe and sound with an endless supply of notes, but by November Franco was clearly getting worse, causing doctors to start a whole new medical regimen.

Kathryn left in the spring of 2007 to take up a new challenging post in Toronto, and right after that Franco was admitted again for still another biopsy. The shocking news given us by our new doctor was that the thirty-five-year-old kidney had suffered acute damage and was working at only 5 percent of its capacity. Franco was put back on dialysis right there and then, and we felt as if we were right back at the beginning with our four-day weeks. And that is why we decided to learn how to do home dialysis—that is, in technical terms, "peritoneal dialysis," because a big tube goes right into the peritoneal cavity, i.e., your belly. After Franco underwent the operation to allow the tube to be connected, we started our training. All during the fall and winter we went to the Faulkner Hospital three days a week to see Terry Moore, our expert nurse and teacher, who also became a dear friend as she helped us adjust to this new life. Then, the day that we passed all our tests, a gigantic crate arrived at our doorstep, and home dialysis began.

Every month the man I call the Baxter man arrived with a truckload of boxes containing masks and tape and rubber gloves and three types of huge bags of liquid marked red, green, or yellow. After checking Franco's numbers each day, we would decide which bag we were supposed to use that day. Long after the machine was taken back, I still have many, many empty Baxter boxes. I have kept them because they are the perfect size for packing and shipping things. And whenever I see the word *Baxter*, I feel a little jolt of remembrance and even nostalgia.

I KNOW THAT several years have passed since Franco died, but there are still some mornings when I look over to his side of the bed and almost expect the machine to still be there. I have no schedule now; I have nobody depending on me for anything. I often feel as if I have no purpose in life. My purpose for years had been: Keep him alive.

Then it comes back to me: the neck brace, the backaches, the tummy aches.

Now I AM doing my neck exercises while taking my walk. The physical therapist told me to turn my head to the left, then to the right, then lean left down onto my shoulder, then down to the right, then look way up and way down. I try to remember to do them every day, even though my neck really doesn't hurt the way it used to. She prescribed these motions for me several years ago, when my neck hurt so much I often had to wear a brace. Every afternoon while Franco took his nap on the couch, I would lie down on the bed with the brace behind my neck for support. I even used a machine for a while that had several vibrating pads attached to it. You'd plug it in and then attach the pads to your neck, and the machine would do a massage on you. Nothing helped. In those days it used to kill me to have to turn my neck in one direction or the other, the worst times being when I was driving and having to look round at the back to see if a car was behind me.

I can't remember exactly when my neck stopped hurting. Franco had been gone for I don't know how many months when I began to realize that it didn't hurt to turn around and look behind me. How could that be? I had always thought that our various aches and pains got worse as we got older, never got better or actually went away. But then people would say to me: "Do you realize the stress you were under during those months and years that Franco was sick and you were taking care of him? You were constantly worrying about him."

Yes, that was my full-time job for a long time, worrying about him and taking care of him. If I could have him back, just the way he was, would I care if my neck hurt or if I got those frequent stomach upsets? It feels terrible to me to be happily rid of neck pain at the expense of his having had to die. A friend says to me: "Don't even go down that path."

She is right. Then I think, *Would he want to be back, having to live that way again?* Maybe that is why he finally left me. Was he thinking: *Enough with tubes and machines and blood drawings and endless pills and injections and surgeries ...*

I am sure that Franco is pleased that my neck pain has gone away.

IN THE SYSTEM

IT STILL HAPPENS, after all this time.

It happened again today at the UPS office where I went to mail a package.

"Are you in our system?" asked the genial clerk.

He tapped some keys on the computer, and there it popped up, Franco's name; he is in the system.

My heart pounded out of my chest at seeing his name, and I found myself holding on to the edge of the counter.

"I'm sorry," I told the clerk, "it's hard for me. Could you please change the name to Gwen?"

Last week I went to the optical shop with my prescription for a new pair of glasses. I gave the optician my name, and he opened up the files in his computer.

"Well, I can't find anything under your name. You must have been here more than three years ago."

"I really can't remember exactly...."

"Here it is, Franco Romagnoli!"

"But he is dead!" I blurted out.

I can't believe I said that. Where did that come from? How could I have said that, right there in that shop with other people around? Sometimes I feel as if I just cannot stand it any more. Franco popping up in machines all over the place, but never really there anymore, never by my side like he used to be.

"He must have been here within three years, because that's how far back my computer files go," said the optician, not really responding to what I had said. Had he not heard me, was he just pretending he hadn't heard me, or was this moment too embarrassing for him? He didn't know what to say to me.

"He died two years ago." I thought if I repeated this information he would react to what I was saying. "You should take him out of the computer; you could just put Gwen in the place of Franco."

Still no response. Then a few moments later a mumbled "I'm sorry."

It takes a lot of courage to go to all those places and have to tell somebody that the Franco on their computers or bank statements or letters or magazines or bills is not here anymore. I am always having to tell people that Franco has died, then watching their lips, as I know they are going to say: "Oh, I am so sorry." Over and over again.

People have to say something, even though they may never have laid eyes on Franco. Even if it did happen more than two years ago, it isn't their fault; how could they have known? It is up to me, the widow, to tell them the news that breaks my heart to say. For them, it is a name on a form, or a window in a computer. Unless, unless, just by chance, this has ever happened to them: the unbearable feeling of losing someone you loved, someone so close to you in life that sometimes you think you are only half a person.

I remember when I had to go to the bank because the checks ran out on our joint checking account, and I needed to order more. I wanted to keep them the same, but the bank manager said he was sorry, but I must order checks with only my name on them. The account should be in my name only, too, and "I will be able to make that change in only a moment." I waited in the chair while he called somebody up on the phone and told someone to please delete the name "Franco" on the account and keep the name "Gwen." Hanging up, he said, "I have taken care of that for you, but it may take several months for the change to show up on the statements. It's in the system, you see, so it takes time. I'm sorry about that."

"I understand." I say. "It's in the system."

They are sorry, I think, not because he died, but because they had to hear my words. They are sorry they ever had to be put in the position of having to say they were sorry—about something they know nothing about.

As time goes on, I find that I am the one feeling sorry, sorry for having placed them in this uncomfortable position, sorry for them instead of for me.

ALL THE THINGS PEOPLE
GIVE ME TO READ

I AM LOOKING once again at my shelf full of books about grieving: books on how to deal with the loss of a spouse, books on the stages of grieving, books that tell you how to mourn, books about counseling, books about drugs, and of course, the ones I call the celebrity books—the ones by Joan Didion, by Joyce Carol Oates, by C. S. Lewis, by Kübler-Ross, and many others given to me by friends during those first months after Franco died.

I received poems that people had written about their own losses, envelopes from people who had inserted an article they'd cut out of some newspaper about how others have coped with loss, emails telling me to go on a website where people talk about how they deal with death in the family. Most of these I couldn't even look at. There was something odd about hearing the sad stories of strangers.

One friend gave me Joan Didion's popular book *The Year of Magical Thinking* just the second week after Franco died. I read a few pages and thought I would collapse, it was so painful. Sometimes it's just too early to read words like that. Recently, I opened the book again, and managed to get through it. It wasn't painful this time; it was more nostalgic, like my having the same feeling about Franco's shoes that she had about her husband's: I have to keep them; he may need them if and when he comes back. So many thoughts were like mine: *Now I have no one to talk to about this, no one to laugh with or discuss anything.*

But I found it hard to get through some parts of the book. I could not relate to her world of famous places and people that she and her husband had known and consorted with … lunch at the Bistro in Beverly Hills … dinner at Morton's … and receiving phone calls from famous prople … She often sounded so literary, but that, of course, is because she is such a fabulous writer. Then not too long after her husband died, she also lost her daughter. It just was too much to fathom. The one sentence that hit me hard, though, and has always stayed with me, was "You sit down to dinner and life as you know it ends," because that is what happened to me. "You go home from the hospital the way you did all those other times, except this time, life as you know it ends."

When Joyce Carol Oates' book, *A Widow's Story*, came out, I found out that she had already gotten married again. It was only about a year after her husband had died, and she had been in the middle of writing a book about her grief. She had had a similar experience to mine—her husband in the hospital, thinking he'd get well, nurses constantly asking about "extraordinary measures," something unexpected happens, and he is suddenly gone. But it's difficult for me to shake the thought in my head: *How could she be writing that emotional story while planning a wedding with another man?* How could someone feel the way she wrote about her husband and get married so soon after he died? Then, I thought, is it possible that when one is married for many years, forty or fifty, say, that a marriage can become routine or shaky? I have friends who've been together for 45 years and bicker all the time. Others seem to just stay together out of habit. Perhaps those marriages become stale and even loveless over time … not always idyllic just because they last for a long time. So, should I then feel blessed about my ten years instead of always wanting more?

The speed at which Joyce Carol Oates wrote her book on grieving the loss of her husband reminded me of the *New Yorker* cartoon that Franco cut out of the magazine for me a long time ago. In the living room, the husband is sitting on a chair, reading the paper, while the wife is at her computer. He says to her: "Joyce Carol Oates seems to have no trouble coming out with book after book."

I KNEW THAT Elisabeth Kübler-Ross had written the so-called seminal account of the stages of accepting one's own death, but a more recent one that I bought myself, called *On Grief and Grieving,* talks about the stages of learning to deal with a loved one's death. It just didn't seem to fit for me, and I found it impossible to follow certain steps that had been laid out by someone else. For me each day might be totally different from the one before: one day I can get up by 8 a.m., I can go out to the gym or meet a friend, and the next day I cannot even slip out from under the bed covers.

THE ONE THAT made the greatest impression of all was C. S. Lewis' *A Grief Observed*. He and Joy, the true love of his life, met late in life, as Franco and I did, and had been married only three years when she died of cancer. Like me, he felt cheated. He had written so much about Christianity and could not accept what people would say to him, just as I can't: She is with God; she is at peace, etc. He kept trying to figure out how Christianity could fit into the loss of his beloved wife.

"The pain now is part of the happiness then. That's the deal," Lewis wrote. Perhaps the only way to explain these things.

A WHILE AGO in the *Boston Globe,* I saw an interview with the author of a new book about grief, touted in a headline as "The Definitive Text on Grieving in Today's World".… Definitive? There is nothing definitive about grieving. Only someone who has never lost someone close or has ever had to experience grief could write a sentence like that one.

And those very thoughts of mine were confirmed when I later read another *Globe* article called "Grief Disorder," by Joan Wickersham, a novelist and columnist who writes regularly for the paper. Her article struck me immediately, because it was about the futility of putting grief into categories. As an example, she mentioned the recent ludicrous proposal by the American Psychiatric Association to identify something called "complicated grief disorder," defined as "intense, acute grief that persists for more than six months after bereavement." I had heard about that myself but never knew the exact definition. And now that I have read it, I can't figure out "six months after bereavement." Is bereavement the day your loved one died? How long is bereavement supposed to be? What is the difference between bereavement and grief?

Joan Wickersham writes: "The rationale is that since most people get over a death in six months (um, excuse me, but who are these people?), the new diagnosis would allow people who struggle with prolonged grief to get treatment... But every grief is different, just as every death and every mourner is different."

I felt compelled to write Ms. Wickersham to thank her for her perceptive words and to tell her that I was paragraph one of her article. This is what she wrote in that paragraph:

"Recently at a cocktail party, I met a woman whose husband had died about four years ago. She mentioned him a lot. Not monologues, but frequent references to him—things he'd said, jokes he'd made, his foibles, his likes and dislikes. Some of it was in the past tense and some in the present." *Clearly,* she thought to herself while listening to the woman, *this marriage is still going on.*

The author was so right, for me, when she said that we should not pathologize mourning; we should let it be whatever it is. And so I say to my friends and acquaintances whom I may have bored and exasperated out of their wits with my reminiscences and references to Franco (though you have kindly never told me so), "It is whatever it is."

TOTALED

I JUST WATCHED a great big salvage truck loaded with battered vehicles tow away my car. It was the Volkswagen Jetta that Franco and I got brand new in 1998, one of the few purchases we made together. We met so late in life that each of us already had most of what we needed, so we didn't have to buy much else. I've been hanging on to our communal goods, but this time I had no choice. The Jetta was totaled.

Totaled was one of those words that always made me curious. I had heard it but never quite figured out what it meant. Now I know.

I had been waiting at a crosswalk where pedestrians were crossing when a huge SUV came from behind and plowed right into the car. I was okay, but the back of our wonderful, reliable car got so smashed in that no auto-body shop would fix it. That's totaled.

I know our Jetta is not so brand new anymore, but it always worked. Hardly ever needing a repair, it just kept on going and going. And it had all those special accoutrements: the bright orange tennis ball that Franco had appended to the top of the radio antenna so we could find the car in a parking lot; the plastic shelf he had fashioned on the passenger side of the dashboard, for placing things like pencils and sunglasses that would otherwise slide onto the floor; and that specially devised container made of straps in the trunk for holding the car documents. I've had to give up those improvements, except, of course, for the antenna with the orange ball. It still resides, along with the fountain, as an art object in the living room.

WHEN WE FIRST met, Franco and I found many similarities between us, one of which was our choice of car. We both had Volkswagens, mine the simple Rabbit and his the slightly more prestigious Golf. Each of our cars had a gearshift and a clutch. He was the only person I knew who also had a manual transmission, both of us believing that it gave us more control when driving. And neither one of us ever locked our car doors—figuring that if someone was going to steal, we much preferred that they do it without breaking a window.

When we decided we needed only one car, we gave the Rabbit to charity, and the Golf got traded in for our new stick-shift Jetta.

I had actually been thinking for a while about buying an automatic car, since I have so much trouble pushing that clutch up and down while sitting in traffic—that's because of the sciatica in my left leg. That's a funny word: *sciatica*. When I was younger and first heard of it, I had no idea what it was except that, like gout, it happened to old people. It's been happening to me for a while, even when Franco was still with me. He would ferry me back and forth to the hospital, first for my back surgery, and then for those periodic steroid shots they put right into my spine. Franco would sit in the room and later tell me that it was the biggest needle he had ever seen in his whole life. I'm glad I didn't have to see it, but those injections helped me for a long time. Now that the sciatica is back again, I think maybe this totaling was meant to be. I won't have to sit in pain in traffic anymore: I am going to get a car with automatic transmission and be just like everybody else.

It's just that I hated to see our car go this way.

I KNOW THAT I am perfectly capable of buying a car by myself, but I will desperately miss Franco's expertise. I remember in 1998, when we went to buy the new car, it seemed that everybody I knew had a Camry, and it felt so cushy. But after Franco drove one, he said, "No, it doesn't hold the road well enough." We checked out several different brands, and after road-testing each one, Franco would say: "You have to feel the car hold the road." That's why we got the Jetta, a Volkswagen being the number-one holder of the road for him. Did I ever feel it hold the road? I had no idea.

After the accident, I drove a rental car for a while, a Chevy Impala that felt large and cushy, but as for holding the road? I still had no idea. One thing I do know is that my left leg kept searching for a clutch that wasn't there, and my right hand kept trying to find second gear. I put my sunglasses on the dashboard on the passenger side, and the first time I had to brake at a light, they fell on the floor.

I START TO look for my replacement car and test-drive three different models, including a Volkswagen. But in the end I am attracted by that bright blue Honda Civic sitting right there on the showroom floor. It's not just blue, my salesman corrects me: it's Dyno Pearl Blue. And I get leather seats. It's cushy, but not large and, as it now runs into its third year, drives beautifully and has never needed a thing. I've learned not to search for a gearshift, my left leg never hurts, and I have no idea whether or not it holds the road.

ANOTHER SPRING

THIS MORNING WHEN I looked out at my terrace, I saw the first buds of spring on the trees. And I heard Nina Simone singing in my head: "I'm thankful for seeing another spring."

Every spring since Franco died, it happens. I have been allowed to see another spring, but not him, and why is that? Why, I ask myself, are many of us seeing another spring and many others are not?

I saw the huge rhodies out on their bushes when I left the house today, some bright pink, others scarlet. The first time I ever said "rhodies" to Franco, he looked at me, bewildered, and then laughed uproariously. He'd never heard rhododendrons called that, but that's what we called them when I was growing up. The magnolias have almost finished their blooming and so has the forsythia, but the azaleas are out in full force.

I go walking again in Mount Auburn Cemetery, but not on a path that's near his stone. I wander instead throughout all the rest of that splendid garden. The birdwatchers are out early each morning now, because these are the days to see more birds than at any other time of year. They have come back from the South, and this is their mating time. I am told by bird enthusiasts that the birds love this place because it is filled with the seeds they like to eat. All along the paths I pass the birders, heads turned up high, eyes planted firmly on their binoculars, peering into the trees in a desperate attempt to see some new species. *Those craning necks are surely going to ache,* I think, *at the end of the day.* The truly serious ones are lugging giant camera lenses, so big and heavy they have to be carried on the photographers' backs in oversize backpacks, or even pushed around on wheeled carts. If Franco were still with me, he'd have his camera with him, too, and he'd be shooting pictures here, as he used to, in every season.

I retrace some of the steps that Franco and I took together: past the monument, past the ponds, and past the mausoleum where almost all the names are Italian, a part of this burial ground that is just like all the cemeteries in Italy. There is not enough space underground in that country, so tall marble walls containing what look like huge drawers are built high up above the ground. Even here I see that, just as in Italy, many of the facades of these crypts are covered with mementos: badges and ribbons and especially photographs—of the loved one and of family members, all taken when they were very young. So that even if the dates show that the person was in her eighties when she died, the photograph is of a young girl in her twenties. I am reminded of the many times that Franco and I were in Rome and I wanted to go to the graves of his parents, but he would never go. He did not want to look at those old photographs of his parents, not representing at all the way he remembered them. He would just keep their pictures in his mind.

FROM MY PATIO I look out on a big oak tree, and beyond that tree, I see the Charles River. Just a few weeks ago I had a total view of the river, when my oak tree was only winter bark and stripped limbs. Then appeared a tiny outcropping of bright green, the tiniest leaves alongside dripping fuzzy appendages. Another glance outside my window and the leaves had gotten big enough to slightly cut my view of the Charles. And now, it seems like no time later, full leaves are swaying in the wind. If you skip just a couple of days, you could miss the whole transformation that tree makes. You would just one day look outside and find only a slice of the river left.

Is it possible that those photos I sent to my grandchildren of my patio piled up with five feet of snow were taken such a short time ago? Will this spring go by as quickly as that winter did?

Suddenly in my mind appears the motto on the T-shirt that man at the health club wears every day, the one that says "Carpe Diem." I always think it looks corny, so why is it floating through my head right now? I guess it is saying to me to savor every moment of this spring season, because it will be gone before you know it. And we never know if we will get to see another spring.

TO DO IT OR NOT TO DO IT

Do I want to keep everything the same way it was, or do I want to change things so that when I look at them, I won't, or I might not, think of him?

Do I want to keep all those letters and brochures and catalogs and notices that come addressed to Franco and just stare at his name, or do I want to throw them away immediately, and try not to remember?

Do I want to keep the closet door open so I can keep looking at his shirts, remembering how they looked on him, remembering the smell that has long gone, or keep the door closed and never look in there again, or finally get up the courage to give them to charity?

Should I have our favorite drink, a negroni, to celebrate the buying of my new car, or never have a negroni again, since I can't ever have one with Franco again?

Should I read that thick, ultra-glossy magazine called *Style* that came again today in the Sunday *New York Times,* or throw it out right away? If I read it, I will immediately feel guilty, knowing that Franco would be saying: "Oh, God, there's that awful *Style* magazine again with those unwearable clothes and the snobbiest pieces of writing I've ever seen." If Franco were here with me this Sunday, the *Style* supplement would have already made its way to the recycling bin, but I am intrigued, so it still sits on the coffee table. Am I being disloyal if I just peek inside and see how bizarre everything is?

It is nearing Christmastime again. Should I buy another live evergreen tree, decorate it with twinkling lights, and place it on the terrace just outside our sliding door, as Franco and I did every year? Then, when holiday time is over, take off the lights and line up the tree on the terrace alongside all the other ones from previous years? I just saw a lovely blue spruce at the plant store. Do I want to buy it for the terrace and decorate it, or do something totally new instead?

Should I keep all those documents from the old Jetta we bought together—the one now totaled—or throw them away? Maybe keep just one?

Should I keep listening to his favorite CD while I am on the treadmill at the health club, or never listen to it again?

Do I want to continue opening his desk drawer and looking at his old eyeglasses, or should I give them to the ophthalmologist so he can recycle them?

Should I change the music on my cell phone so as not to be reminded of all those calls to and from doctors and hospitals? Or is there something comforting about remembering in spite of the pain it brings?

Some people say, "Why don't you change your email address from "gwenfranco" now that so much time has passed?" Maybe I like to look at our two names together, but would I feel better if I changed it?

Do I want to keep his toolboxes just the way they were, not disturbing even one nail or screwdriver, wire, or pot of glue, or should I give them all away to someone who could use them?

The first spring after Franco died, I looked out onto our terrace that he loved so much and heard him say: "Look, a red hibiscus has just come out." Should I plant the very same flowers he did, or plant totally different flowers in brand new pots, or do nothing at all, and just leave the terrace bare?

Do I want to keep his old cell phone, his 1999 Toshiba laptop, the uncorrected proofs of his book, his old cameras, the mirror on the wall for the home dialysis machine, his instruction sheet for the dialysis machine, or should I throw it all in the trash?

Should I keep all those old colored slides of all his travels, buy a scanner, scan them, and put them on a CD, or just realize that they are terribly faded, that nobody is going to look at them, and just throw them away?

Should I keep using his handkerchiefs with the monogrammed *R* on them, or get rid of them?

Should I keep all those photographs of him displayed in all the rooms of this place, or put them away—at least some of them, anyway?

Do I want to keep that folder full of those surreptitious love notes he used to fax me in my office when I was still working? Or throw them away before they are left for my son to deal with?

Do I ever want to make gnocchi verdi again, the recipe that introduced my son to Franco before he became Sean's stepfather, when Sean called to ask him how to make them?

Do I want to keep the license plates from the totaled car, the ones that had "FD" on them, which we said stood for "Franco the Driver"? Or do I want to get new ones?

Do I want to go to the trouble of making one of his favorite dishes for dinner, or just keep on enjoying my roasted cauliflower and Brussels sprouts, which I know he wouldn't eat?

How much remembering do we want to do? How much remembering causes us pain and how much causes us joy?

NAMES

I SENT BACK the WBUR notice requesting a donation with a note saying, "Please change the address from 'Franco and Gwen Romagnoli' to only 'Gwen Romagnoli.'" I had done that several times before, but nobody seemed to pay attention, so the notices kept coming with both names.

Until today. The letter that arrived from the radio station was addressed to "Gwen" all by herself. I felt a shock; I really wasn't sure I wanted to see my name all alone, after all. *Gwen, I said to myself, you can't have it both ways. Try to think: Which way would be better for you?*

I know my email still says "gwenfranco," but I can't think of what I'd change it to. And I know that the people who write me are saying to themselves, *Shouldn't she change that?*

When I went to vote, there was my name, all alone, on the voting sheet at my street address. I wanted to see his name there. Who took it away?

When Franco—whose birth name was Giovanni Francesco, which was then reduced to Gian Franco or Gianfranco—first came to the U.S. from Italy, he discovered that nobody knew how to say Gian. (It is actually pronounced exactly the way its English counterpart is pronounced: "John.") So he decided he would go by Franco, a name people didn't seem to have any trouble with. But so as not to totally lose his real name, he started to write "G. Franco Romagnoli." And that is the way it stayed all his life.

Except that there are all these notices that arrived, and continue to arrive, addressed to Franco G., because nobody seemed to be able to deal with an initial that came first rather than second. And I wondered how the famous trial lawyer managed: F. Lee Bailey. Did his mail always come addressed to Lee F.? What about W. Somerset Maugham, or J. Edgar Hoover? There was a movie called just *J. Edgar.* The title doesn't even need his last name, because everybody knows who J. Edgar was. I kind of doubt that his mail was ever misaddressed.

WHAT TO DO about the paralyzed veterans? Franco gave them money once, so they keep writing back and sending whole envelopes full of those return-address stickers printed with his name and an American flag, or sometimes a big bald eagle.

"Oh," my friend Catherine said, "for those just write in big letters 'DE-CEASED' on the envelope and send it right back. That way you will never hear from them again."

The word, *deceased,* I can't even bear to hear her say it, let alone write it myself anywhere. But then, her husband has been dead for twelve years, so maybe it has become easier for her to say out loud words like *deceased.* I send the paralyzed veterans a check instead.

It's a postal world of already-printed-out-labels, and those labels stay in the system forever, never changing. Even in death. There isn't any human writing with a pen any more.

Then there is the question: How should people write to me? Am I Mrs. Franco, or Mrs. Gwen, or just plain Gwen, or am I now a Ms. once again? Probably not a Miss, I would guess. My mother's *Emily Post's Etiquette,* the 1929 edition of which I inherited, says, "Correctly and properly a widow keeps her husband's name for *always.*"

Emily goes on to say, "According to best taste, no note or social letter should ever be addressed to a married woman—even if she is a widow—as Mrs. Mary Town. Best taste and truth agree that the man gave his name when he gave the wedding ring—both were for life, or until the woman marries again."

So I guess that means the Boston Symphony Orchestra is correct in sending its mail addressed to "Mrs. Franco Romagnoli." But what about my sister, who writes to me as "Mrs. Gwen Romagnoli"? And all those who write "Ms.," of course, though Emily Post could never have known about that.

FRANCO, I HAVE SO MANY
THINGS TO TELL YOU

I'VE BEEN THINKING, Franco, about all the things that you don't know, the many things that have happened since you left. So much to tell you ...

ITALY

ONE OF THE Italian movies that passed through Boston not too long ago was called in English *I Am Love*. I have to see them all, whether reviews are good or bad, because it is so rare I get to see a movie in Italian. The cinematography was incredible, but I know that you would have complained because the movie was so slow. Still, I know you would have appreciated the beautiful scenery; after all, you were a filmmaker once. And guess what? Gabriele Ferzetti is in it, now 85 years old, one of your childhood playmates in your Rome neighborhood, except you said he was called Pasquale then. He was handsome, though, so when some agent picked him up for the movies, they gave him the name Gabriele, much more urbane and sophisticated compared to Pasquale, that southern, even Sicilian, name. It's true, as you said, he can't act to save his life. Luckily, it was Antonioni who cast him in films like *L'Avventura* and *L'Eclisse,* where all he had to do was stand around and look pretty for the camera.

And there are other things to tell you about Italy. For some reason, I have become a recipient of newsletters from the Italian consulate in Boston. I think a new consul general has arrived, because you and I never used to receive such a big flurry of announcements. It is about the 150th anniversary of the unification of Italy. I remember when you used to talk to me about the 100th in 1961, such an important event because before 1861, think of it, Italy was just a big peninsula of separate city-states. There was no Italy then as we know it now; hard to believe your "old country" is younger even than the United States. Well, the consul general informs me that there is going to be a grand event to celebrate the unification, happening right here in Boston. All the Italians of Boston may be gathering right at this moment at the State House for speeches and libations. Would we have gone if you were here?

Recently there was a huge earthquake in the Abruzzi region—you won't believe it. It totally destroyed our favorite hotel in L'Aquila, the Duca degli Abruzzi. How many times did we stay there on our way from Rome to Le Marche? So many, I can't even count. You wouldn't believe the photo I saw of the hotel after the quake: just rubble, including that beautiful rooftop restaurant where we'd always order the *tonnarelli della perdonanza,* the pasta with saffron, which made the whole dish look like gold.

Italy's politics are getting even crazier than ever. They had an election and the person who got the most votes is a comedian called Beppe Grillo, a very funny guy and obviously very smart. And we thought in the past that things couldn't get any worse!

FAMILY AND FRIENDS

FRANCO, BELIEVE IT or not, Sean and Hannah have been married for nineteen years! I met you just months before their wedding and dragged you all over Newburyport looking for the right place for a rehearsal dinner. I made you try the food at so many places, because you were the expert. I did all that to you after knowing you for only four months, and you were so obliging. Just think, if you were alive now, we would know each other for more than nineteen years!

Remember when your granddaughter Katie stayed with us for a few months when she was 4? She's already graduated from college! And from Smith; she's a smartie. And Marco's daughter, gorgeous Francesca, has graduated from Fordham, lives in Greenwich Village (just as I did a millennium ago), and has a really interesting job. Second son Marco just had his sixtieth birthday, and that means that your number-one son, Gian, is a couple of years older than that. And I am staggered at the realization that your stepson, Sean, will turn 50 this year. I am right here on this earth, in touch with many of these offspring, and even I find it overwhelming to realize how fast these kids and grandkids grow up. So I can imagine what it must be like for you to absorb this quick passage of the years. Sean's little Evie tells me she just had her eight-and-three-quarters birthday, and she was only two when you died. I do so wish you could see this sassy, sharp, bright, and beautiful girl right now. Rory tells me he still remembers you, Babbo; he was five the last time you saw him, but now a tall, willowy sports nut and math genius at age 12.

The last time I was in Italy, it was four years ago, and the only time I have been back without you. I took some of your ashes with me, and Sean and I let them fly into the waters of the Tiber. I know you would have approved. It was a mixed trip this time, because just before I arrived your grandnephew, that lovely boy Luca, was killed on his *motorino*. He was only 17. Your sister, his grandmother, Mirella, was devastated, of course, not to mention Simona and Nico, the parents. I have known them for years, ever since you first took me to Rome to meet your family, and they all felt part of my own family. What a sweet boy he was, Luca, a champion sailor, and the last time you and I saw him he was only 10. Sean and Hannah and the children came over for a while, too, and we stayed in a nice apartment in the quiet part of Trastevere. I am now planning a mother-son road trip with Sean, starting in Rome and driving to Milano, Torino and then through France as a fiftieth birthday present for him. I'll be sure to visit Mirella and the rest of our Roman family.

And here is news I know would make you happy: our wonderful agent, Joy, gave birth to her first child, a son, four years ago on December

15, the day you died. It felt as if a new life was meant to come into the world the date you left it.

WRITING

FRANCO, REMEMBER THAT first piece I wrote for the Coupling column in the *Boston Globe* about what name to call you? You were too old for me to call you "boyfriend," so I came up with a bunch of other names, like paramour, consort (Hannah's choice), beau, etc. I am just realizing that you have never read any of the other columns I have written for that page in the magazine section, now called Connections. There have been ten more, and all of them since you've been gone. It is breaking my heart that I am working on a book about your dying and my being a widow. Instead we might have written another book together. Remember we were going to write that book about the Le Marche region of Italy? I sometimes wonder whether I should do it myself, but it wouldn't be the same without you. And then there is still my proposal for the book called *Gray Love* ... about people like us meeting and falling in love later in life. I miss that you are not here to read everything I write, the way you used to. And I used to read all your writing, and even with the disagreements, we'd help each other. You were my best critic.

A JOB

ANOTHER THING YOU don't know is that I have been working at Stellina Restaurant on Friday nights as an assistant hostess. It is my one day to dress up and wear the beautiful jewelry you gave me. Ginnie taught me everything I need to know about the job, and I have become quite experienced. I am especially good at being pleasant when people come in the door; I am good at taking them to their seats and waiting for them to sit down before I place the menus in front of them. I am somewhat proficient at ringing up the checks at the front desk until there are a ton of people waiting for them; then I tend to get a bit flustered. I have to admit, though, that no matter how much I try, I have a terrible time remembering which table has which number. So when Ginnie says, "Take this party of four to table twenty-one," I have to close my eyes and try to see the seating chart in my mind's eye. I am fine from numbers one to fifteen, though I sometimes get some of them backwards, but above that, it is often a challenge. Sometimes Ginnie will just have to nudge me and whisper in my ear, "That big table by the front window." After all, I only work once a week, and I have never been too great with numbers. But I love my job and have such a good time being out and about, seeing people, many of whom are old friends of yours and mine. Lots of them stop and like to talk to me about you. After we close, I sit at the bar, have a glass of wine, and picture you waiting for me there in the corner seat of table three, my favorite.

WATERTOWN, MASSACHUSETTS

FRANCO, HOW TO begin to describe what has happened to your adopted hometown of Watertown, Mass. It has become famous, all due to a horrible tragedy that occurred during the Boston Marathon a couple of years ago.

I actually found out that our town had become infamous when the telephone rang at 8 a.m. on Friday, April 19, 2013. It was our friend Chris, calling from Rome. "How are you?" she asked with a frantic tone in her voice. "Are you all right?"

Because she lives in Europe and had already had five hours of news-watching, she knew that two suspected terrorists were hiding somewhere in Watertown, and that they were being called "armed and dangerous" by the police.

I had originally learned what the accused might have done when I turned on my car radio as I was leaving the accountant's office on the afternoon of April 15, having filed my taxes at the last minute as usual. The reporter said that somebody had planted two bombs at the finish line of the marathon and that many people had been seriously injured. As soon as I got home, I naturally turned on the TV and started to watch the news unfold. Only hours later did I realize that I had not yet taken off my coat. As I watched, I kept remembering how we huddled together on the couch as we watched the events of 9/11 unfold so many years before. Here was another pristine blue-sky day, another day of anxiety, of fear and helplessness, as I watched horrible things happen that I could do nothing to stop. But so different this time, hard to be all by myself with no one's arm across my shoulders, no one to share the sadness with, just to be a presence in the room with me.

Your town became known everywhere four days later, when the two brothers suspected of leaving backpacks containing pressure cookers at the finish line fled to the little suburban streets of Watertown. The next day the edict came down from the State House that all of us in the Boston area were to be in a sense quarantined; that is, no one was allowed to go out of the house. Coincidentally, Sean and Hannah and Rory and Evie had come here the day before to help me celebrate my birthday. And so, here we were, cooped up inside with a six- and nine-year-old who would have much preferred to go to the park. We played some Simon Says and a lot of our favorite card game, Uno, while Sean and I tried to watch developments on TV at the same time, attempting to shield the news from the children.

The next day we were permitted to go out, because one of the brothers had been killed and the younger one discovered and arrested. That brother was severely wounded, but has survived and, in fact, is on trial right now in Boston.

My sister, who as you know lives in Pennsylvania, said that whenever her friends would ask her where her sister lived, she would say, somewhere outside of Boston. But now she will just say that her sister lives in Watertown, Massachusetts, and everybody will know what that is.

Who would have thought, Franco, that your adopted hometown would become not just famous, but infamous?

WHAT WOULD HE
LOOK LIKE NOW?

THE ELDERLY MAN is pedaling as best he can on the stationary bicycle in the health club, accompanied by a home health aide who watches his every move. I do a double take, and my heart begins to pound.

This man could be Franco if he had lived to the age of 90. The same beard mixed gray and brown, the same spotty hair on top of a mostly bald head, the same eyeglasses, the shape of his face ... except this face has a lot of those brown spots that Franco's didn't have yet, a face thinner than Franco's, but a face that could have been his had he lived, say, eight years more. I can't take my eyes off the face of this man. His caregiver, a young blonde woman, sits on the next bicycle and doles out little pieces of something for him to eat ... are they pills? Candy? I am not close enough to see.

There are several other older men who come here, accompanied by health care assistants who always sit patiently nearby and monitor every movement as the men pedal ever so slowly, but this is the first time I have seen one who so resembled Franco. This man is hunched over and not as robust as Franco had been even when he was sick, but eight more years ... I wonder how I would be if I had taken care of Franco for eight more years, until he was 90. Would I have had the strength and stamina for that? It was hard work and often wore me out, but I miss the caretaking. After he was gone, for a long time I felt as if there was nothing for me to do all day. I am much better now that some years have passed, but I still remember how those long days just stretched out before me.

I think about those sad photos of the missing children that used to be on the milk cartons. There would be the picture of the child when abducted and then another picture drawn by an artist that showed what that child would look like now, maybe as many as ten years later. I wonder who the artists are who are able to do that transformation; if I could find one, I would ask him to draw me a picture of Franco.

I CANNOT KEEP from glancing over at the man on the bicycle, trying to look more closely at the details of his eyeglasses. I still have a pair of Franco's glasses in my drawer, not ready yet to give them away. I finally did give the other pair to the eye doctor because he recycles them, but I just couldn't do it all at once.

The man has finished pedaling and slowly gets up off the seat, bent and fragile. He turns toward the young woman, who carefully puts his jacket on for him. I wonder how old he really is. Franco always looked younger than his years, at least that's what everybody said.

I think, *What if?* What if Franco had never gotten sick with kidney disease? What if the transplant had not failed? What if he hadn't had to go back on dialysis? What if he had been healthy enough to walk up the stairs by himself without my holding on to him and pushing him up one step at a time? I stop and do not say "What if" again to myself. I hear my friend's voice saying to me once again: "Don't even go down that path."

I REMEMBER WHAT my father used to do. He, too, always looked much younger than his age. When he was still able to get out and about, he would constantly ask people: "How old do you think I am?" and when they would say, "Oh, about 75," his face would light up with pride as he told them, "I'm 99!" He lived to be 101. I muse on whether I could ever possibly be so proud of being old.

Back at the health club a few days later, I once again see the man who could be Franco at 90. He doesn't look frail enough to be in a nursing home, and then, would a person in a nursing home come to a health club, even with an aide? Perhaps it's assisted living, or could it be he lives alone? He is on the bicycle again with the caregiver at his side. When he is finished, she gently helps him off the bike and down the corridor to another machine. He holds on tightly to her arm.

Would Franco be holding tightly onto my arm if he were 90 and we were taking a walk? I know he would, because he was already holding onto me all those years after he got sick. He'd be more frail now, but I'd still have him.

THE BELLS OF ROME

You don't know, Franco, that at this very moment the eyes of the world are focused on your native city. Something has happened that you could not imagine, nor could anybody else: the pope has resigned. I thought of you as I watched the video of Pope Benedict XVI's last speech from his window in Piazza San Pietro. All the bells of Rome were ringing and ringing and ringing, for what seemed like hours. And I remember all those days when we walked together in Rome and listened to those same bells and felt our deep love for that city.

That's why you named your book about Rome, *A Thousand Bells at Noon*. Just think what a chapter could be added now to that book. "A Pope Resigns": an event that has not occurred for more than 500 years!

*   *   *

It was the year 2000. Franco and I celebrated the millennium in our favorite city, all due to a publisher's love of that city. Just a few months earlier, Franco had been contacted by the publisher and editor of Steerforth Press, a new independent publishing house located in a little town in Vermont. Back in the 1970s, Thomas Powers, a Pulitzer Prize-winning journalist and the founder of Steerforth, had been the editor of the English-language newspaper of Rome: *The Rome Daily American*. He had always wanted to write a book about Rome, or have somebody else write that book, and now that he had his own company, he could do just that. He chose Franco after having read articles that Franco had written about Italy in various magazines and, of course, because Franco is a native Roman.

We arrived in Rome in November 1999 and moved into the sublet apartment in Trastevere that a good friend had found for us. We had to walk up five flights of stairs to get to it, but we could do that in those days. Once there, we found a crowded flat with a small living room, a tiny kitchen, a bedroom, and a little room that Franco would use as his study. The real glory of the place was its gigantic terrace, which was reached from a circular staircase in the living room and from which we could see almost all the cupolas of the city ... and where we could also hang out our laundry and eat our meals, even in the winter.

Franco immediately started on his search throughout Rome for signs of what it was like to live in Rome nowadays, as opposed to almost fifty years before, when he left it to come live in America. Every day he was out in the city interviewing people from all walks of life and who held all kinds of jobs. One day it was a meeting with the head of the city's water-works; another it was visiting the fountains with the woman in charge of the preservation of those splendors; still another he'd be with a funeral director, a priest, a journalist, a transport authority, or a doctor at a local hospital. From all that came chapters on the health system in Rome; faith in Rome; the monuments; the food markets and restaurants; the elaborate water system and the aqueducts; the little fountains found on every street called *nasoni*, little noses, where everybody stops to get a drink; Cinecittà, where so many famous movies have been made; and of course, the government, or its nonexistence, as many critics would say.

When Franco was out each day discovering something else he wanted to write about, I would sometimes accompany him, but other times I'd wander around myself. And little by little I found myself wanting to write about all the aspects of Rome that I knew from my earlier years living there, as well as things that had changed during those twenty-some years.

That is when my own so-called writing career began, my first article, on the *trattorie* of Trastevere, being published by the *Boston Globe* and *Los Angeles Times* Sunday travel sections. I was so new at writing that I sent that same article to both newspapers at the same time, something I was soon told was a no-no. Luckily, both papers published the article on the same Sunday, figuring they were on opposite coasts and that shouldn't do any harm. After that, Franco and I wrote together about places in the regions of Le Marche and Emilia-Romagna, where we made side trips with our numerous visitors from the States.

During our eight-month stay, we made new friends together and each renewed our friendships with old friends from years past. Franco had a group of high school buddies who, believe it or not, after all these many, many years, still got together every Friday night at a local trattoria to have supper. For me that was extraordinary—not just once a month or once a year, but every single week. It was the first time I had met these friends, and we ended up spending many a Friday evening with them, eating fabulous Roman food and drinking more than our share of wonderful local wine.

My name was still on the second-floor bell at the Trastevere apartment where I had lived in the 1970s with my young son, when I worked at the NBC News office. I had left that flat in 1976, when I returned to the States to live, but nobody had ever bothered to change the name. That small building of just three stories had now undergone extensive renovations, each floor having become a condo and up for sale at an astronomically high price. The nostalgia I have for the seven years of my life lived in that apartment has never left me, and I felt compelled to pass that doorway as many times as I could during my stay in Rome in 2000.

That memorable apartment was located just one block off of Piazza Santa Maria in Trastevere, the heart of the district. It was the piazza where everybody converged for the late afternoon *passeggiata* around and around the fountain, where little boys kicked soccer balls in the corner by the church, where we sat for hours at our favorite bar, Bar Marzio, sipping a Campari soda and watching the sun set. And where the big bell of the Santa Maria church tolled every quarter-hour of the day and night—once for the number of the hour, then one bong at quarter past, two at half past, and three at the three-quarter hour. Luckily, I lived just far enough away so that I could hear the grand sound of the bell just slightly, knowing that it was there but never bothered by its loud volume. But those who lived in the buildings surrounding the piazza heard that clanging every fifteen minutes of their lives, all of them so thankful when the pealing of 12:45, day or night, had finished, because the next would be only one toll.

On the night of December 31, 1999, around 11 p.m., Franco and I and a group of our friends congregrated on our terrace with bottles of champagne, awaiting the much-heralded Roman fireworks that were to usher in the new millennium. For a long time preceding that night, we had been told by many journalists, computer experts, and other pundits that we could expect the world to end, or at least crash, that night, due to the Y2K bug. The talk had been going on all over the city, so now we waited not only for the celebration but also for the possibility of world's end.

At midnight we popped open the champagne and watched the splendid fireworks that had been promised, but didn't see the end of the world as we know it. Instead, every bell in the city of Rome began to toll and toll and toll for what seemed like hours.

A THOUSAND BELLS at Noon was published in 2002, with the subtitle, *A Roman Reveals the Secrets and Pleasures of His Native City.* It has been called by critics "the musings of a native son upon returning fifty years later; a story of today's Rome pulsating with life; a small masterpiece; a memoir, a history, a savvy insider's guide and a smart piece of reportage that's as wise, spirited and deep-hearted as the eternal city itself."

Franco's last book—the one I wrote about earlier in this book, the one whose manuscript I found in his desk drawer, his memoir about growing up under Fascism and the Second World War, is called *The Bicycle*

Runner: A Memoir of Love, Loyalty and the Italian Resistance. The final galleys of that memoir were sent from the publisher and handed to me by the postman the day Franco died in December 2008. It was published in 2009.

The final chapter takes place on the Pincio, part of the Villa Borghese that overlooks Piazza del Popolo. Franco and his friend Fred are leaning on the marble balustrade on a Sunday in September, taking in the magnificent sight of the many cupolas, towers, and monuments of Rome. Saint Peter's Basilica "dents the horizon with its presence and dominates it."

Franco writes:

> Exactly at noon, from the Gianicolo Hill across town, the old cannon will boom, and in a moment, as if at a starter's gun, all the church bells will let loose, calling and answering each other, making a joyful noise that, once heard, will not soon be forgotten. Thousands of birds give body to the sound, circling the air, rising and diving and rising again. The pealing is bounced back by the seven hills; here are the bells of Santa Maria Maggiore, and there of San Giovanni in Laterano, and then of San Paolo Fuori le Mura, of Sant'Andrea, of Aracoeli, and above them all *il Campanone*, the Big Bell. It is said that only a Roman, wherever and forever, will recognize the deep, sonorous, majestic voice of Saint Peter's bell: it makes the sky vibrate so that it will reach not only his ears but his heart.

Il Campanone and all the other church bells have rung again, Franco, this time with even more gusto, because a new pope has been elected. As Pope Francis (Papa Francesco to you) gave his homily from St. Peter's Square, his voice was almost drowned out by the pealing of all those glorious Roman bells.

A MEMORIAL

I AM GOING to a memorial service today, Franco, for somebody you don't know, somebody I met at the adult education center after you died. It's at the Quaker Meeting House in Cambridge, so I know the ceremony will be very quiet; at Quaker meetings people just get up to speak when they feel like it. Otherwise, there is silence.

We had a memorial service for you, too, on February 1, your first birthday after your death. It was at the chapel at Mount Auburn Cemetery, and the place was overflowing with family, friends, and acquaintances—those very close to you and others who just wanted to pay respects. Many people got up to speak at your service, too. Some of your children and grandchildren talked about you, and so did Sean. He thanked you for making me, his mother, so happy for those twelve years we had together. Our agent, Joy, talked about your huge talent and the happiness she felt in finding a publisher for your wonderful memoir. John spoke about how he knew you from your television program and then helped you to get your restaurant started. Paul flew all the way from Montana to pay tribute. Rosalind brought one of your wire sculptures to show everyone—that one of the knight and his lady on a horse that you gave her for her wedding. Paolo felt nostalgia for those many evenings when he would sit on the cellar stairs, watching you tinkering with your rows and rows of tools and making the most surprising objects. There were many more who stood up that day and spoke about how much you meant to them.

Still others came up to me after the service to tell me how much they loved your TV show *The Romagnoli's Table*—how much fun they had watching you make all those great Italian meals, and how funny you were, and such a delight. Others told me that they have all your cookbooks, their pages well covered with oil and grease, so heavily used have they been over the years. Not to mention those who discovered real Italian food for the first time at your restaurant.

But the tributes most cherished for me were those that spoke of your whimsical and witty self, your incredible feat of writing whole books in a language not your native one, the wonderful products of your amazing tinkering ability, like the wire sculptures and the fountain made of stuff you found in the basement, and the beautiful portrait photographs you had taken, things like that.

I have been to many funerals and memorial services since you died, Franco, and you don't even know it. Your good friend, Tom, such a lovely man, died a year after you did; he was 89. He had been frail for a long time, much more than you ever were, and yet he lived seven years more than you did. His funeral was at St. Paul's Catholic Church—where you would have expected it to be. He was a devout Catholic and went to church there every Sunday. You and I went to that church together some years ago for his wife's funeral, so, of course, I saw many old friends again at Tom's service. I only met Tom after I met you, and it seemed so strange to be at his funeral without you.

Our dear friend and neighbor, Judy, died, too, and she hadn't yet even reached the age of 70. One night at home she just suddenly fell down from a heart attack, such a shock. Her funeral was a Jewish one, so I attended that one just two days after she was gone.

Then there was Jonathan, our psychiatrist friend. You know, it turns out he had kidney problems, too, and had been on dialysis. So I can trace all the steps to his death. His memorial service was quite impressive, with the large auditorium filled with doctors and other scientific colleagues from all over.

Our friend Werner died when he fell off a ladder at his house when he was trying to clean the eaves. Such a tragic happening, and he not even 70 yet either.

And in Italy, as I told you, Luca died at 17, riding his *motorino* and not wearing a helmet. It is much easier for me to tell you about the deaths of your old school friends—Uccio and your brother and your brother-in-law and Bruno, Sergio, and his brother the doctor, Maria Silvia, your sister-in-law—because they were all our age.

Just recently, another death, Anthony Lewis—you know who he is, the *New York Times* writer, Pulitzer Prize winner, wonderful chronicler of the legal and judicial systems. He was just about your age. I used to see him in the Star Market in Cambridge, looking frail and hunched over while pushing his grocery cart. Ever the gentleman, he would smile and acknowledge me when I would say, like some silly groupie: "Oh, Mr. Lewis, it is so nice to see you," or "I am such a fan of your writing."

How many funerals or memorial services have I been to since you died? Too many, many too many. And just think, some of them for people you had not even met, people I have met since you died. And now that I am getting older myself, I think about these ceremonies more and more often. And you know what I want, Franco? And I've said this to Sean—I would like to have my memorial service while I am still alive, so I can celebrate together with my friends, instead of their waiting to celebrate without me. And it isn't what you think: It's not because I want to know what people will say about me—because obviously if they know I am there they'll probably say only nice things—it's because I want to be with all of them, just be together one last time before I go. It would be like a big party.

And that is sort of how it was after your service, when we all went to Stellina Restaurant for lunch—Stellina, where you and I had so many wonderful dinners with our dear friends Ginnie and Frank, the owners.

A bunch of your old Roman friends were at the memorial, too, and they sang Italian songs for everybody. Ginnie and Frank made all your favorite dishes—even tripe! Or I should say, especially tripe! Everyone had a grand time drinking toasts to you, telling wild stories about your life, and singing those raucous Roman songs.

I wish you could have been at your memorial service, Franco. I think you would have liked it.

Epilogue

LEARNING TO BE a widow means learning to eat dinner alone; learning to buy a single ticket for a movie; learning to hear only silence where there used to be two people talking in your house; learning to go out the door and take a walk by yourself; learning to see only your name on the doorbell, on the email, on the bankbook; learning to get used to the empty chair next to yours; learning to do the errands alone; and learning to say the word *widow* without any tears. It is, after all, called learning for a reason: Learning will go on to become acceptance of your new status, remembering your loved one with joy instead of grief, and being everthankful for the gift you were once given.

I think there is hope in our exchanging our stories with others. We understand each other and share our grief, but this sharing will also help us little by little to overcome that grief and adjust, maybe even happily, to our new lives.

The learning will eventually be like a reflection of this quotation sent to me by a reader:

"Grief is like the wake behind a boat; it starts out as a huge wave that follows close behind you and is big enough to swamp and drown you if you suddenly stop moving forward. But if you do keep moving, the big wake will eventually dissipate. And after a long enough time, the waters of your life get calm again, and that is when the memories of those who have left begin to shine as bright and enduring as the stars above."

THIS EBBING OF the huge wave began to happen to me only recently, several years after Franco's death, and caused me to realize that there could be a life to be lived after Franco.

After Franco

DECEMBER 15 HAS come and gone seven times since that early morning when I called Sean to tell him that Franco had died.

And each time that date would arrive, I'd think, *Could it be he has been gone for so long?*

Gradually, you notice that as those years pass, one by one, the pain begins to ease:

You stop gathering up his clothes in the closet and pressing them close to your face to see if his smell is still there;

You find you're not crying anymore when you look at that special photo of the two of you, or listen to the music you both loved;

You give away his favorite corduroy trousers to Goodwill and recycle his glasses at the optometrist's;

You stop putting out the second place mat on the dining room table;

You don't wince anymore when you see his name come up on the computer at the doctor's office;

You stop carrying his obituary around in your purse;

You respond to mail that still comes in his name and are able to write the words: "My husband has died."

THEN ONE DAY, the unexpected can happen: You find yourself attracted to somebody else.

I had already had my late-in-life mate, so I never ever dreamed there would be another time around for love.

I saw him first in the poetry class I signed up for at the Adult Education Center in Boston. I was amazed at how much he knew about Yeats, so I understood why the teacher was always calling on him. She asked him to stand up and read a poem, and when he recited "The Lake Isle of Innisfree" from memory, I was hooked. I wished I could do that. I listened intently and wondered if the teacher had chosen this student for his interesting accent. But what accent? Is he Irish? No, that couldn't be. My first set of in-laws were from the old country itself, and I surely knew a real Irish brogue if I heard one. Still, there was a tinge of something different, and since I like to think of myself as a student of languages, accents, and grammar, I thought I ought to be able to figure it out. His voice sounded somewhat different when he recited the poem from when he just talked in class, and I wondered, *Is he himself a poet? Does he do readings in public?* I somehow needed to find out, sort of like in *My Fair Lady* when Henry Higgins, in the flower market outside Covent Garden in London, is able to tell each person there exactly where he came from and even where he went to school just because of the way he talked.

At our ten-minute break, I took the empty seat next to his and asked him where he was from. Columbus, Ohio, was definitely not the answer I was expecting. It was a bit like another of my favorite movies, the one that says: "Of all the gin joints in all the towns in all the world, she has to walk into mine." Once a city in which I had no interest whatsoever, Columbus, Ohio, was now the hometown of the most important person to me in the world: my son, who is a professor at Ohio State. For more than seven years, it has been the city to which I travel most, especially now that I have two rapidly growing grandchildren living there.

He is the only person at the center who grew up in Columbus, Ohio, and I am definitely the only person at our school who travels several times a year to visit that city. And all that intrigue about his accent was simply something I should have caught immediately: nothing more exotic than a midwestern accent, like that of my good friend, Lynne from Michigan. They all say "Mondee" and "Tuesdee," instead of "Monday" and "Tuesday," like we easterners do.

We met again after class, and the few words we had exchanged during the break flowed seamlessly into a long conversation about our lives, our families, our interests. It felt to me as if we could have talked for hours about anything at all, and in fact, we did. I found out he'd been divorced for ten years and had three children, two of whom had attended the same school that my son did. I learned that, although he was a lawyer by profession, his true loves were art and literature, and especially poetry. This ability to talk so easily with a man I had barely met was an experience unique for me. We had both lived long lives before that day, so clearly, there was a lot to talk about. We agreed to have lunch soon after to continue our conversation, and we haven't stopped since.

And so, I have both Columbus, Ohio, and William Butler Yeats to thank for giving me the opportunity and desire to go on with a life I never thought would be possible again after the death of Franco.

Especially given my age, I have to say. A late-in-life second marriage for each of us, Franco and I had twelve wonderful years together, happy and amazed that we had found each other. The shadows began to fall, though, not more than four years after we met, upon his diagnosis of kidney failure. Our lives were monumentally altered. More trips to doctors and hospitals began to happen than trips to the movies. When he died, some would say to me that overused but well-meaning phrase: "Wasn't it a blessing, a blessing that he didn't have to suffer anymore?" That I didn't have all that burden of caring for him, the anxiety, the worry? Who knows? Maybe they were right, but back then I felt as if I could have done it forever.

Still, I considered myself lucky. I had never expected to get married again and start a new life. So, after Franco died, I didn't spend much time thinking about a love life. Actually I didn't spend any time at all thinking about it. I stayed for a few months in Columbus in an apartment near my son's house so I could spend more time with my grandkids. It was a compelling attraction to just stay and live there permanently, but all my friends were back in Boston. The life I had built for myself since returning from my life in Italy, it was all here.

I suddenly found that Match.com appeared on my inbox. My friend Mary Lou had decided it was time for me to start over once again. I would look at the pictures of all those old men and think, *Do I really want to do that again?* Nobody ever looked appealing. There were all those brown spots on their faces, those sagging stomachs, clothes that had no style. They tried hard, I know, with their photos: nuzzling the silky collie dog, cuddling with cute little grandkids, leaning against the mast on their sailboat, wearing hiking boots as they trudged up Mount Washington ... all to show the women how active they still were, how endearing they were to their offspring.... What a find they would be!

Was it too soon? Or was it simply that none of them appealed to me? Another woman told me that she checked out men on Cupid-dot-something and that might suit me better. And still another friend actually found her late-in-life mate on one of the sites whose name I can't remember. A major success story, she is now married to her beau, and all the Facebook photos show the two of them looking rapturously happy together. So, "you see," my friends would say to me.

Once I tried, I really did. I think it was Match, not sure, but this guy emailed and asked to take me out. We met at my local diner, noted for its great brunches. As I approached, I could tell it was he waiting outside, partly because I'd seen his photo, but mostly because he was the only older, gray-haired person there. We had scarcely ordered our food when he leaned across the table, peered as closely as he could into my eyes, and said, "I have to be straight and up front with you. I don't want just any old relationship with a woman. I want a romantic one; I want sex. And if you aren't willing for that, then we have nothing more to say."

Well, there I was, having had a hard enough time getting up the courage just to meet some unknown man to eat scrambled eggs with that I must have looked stupefied. I think I stuttered something like, "I'm sorry, but this is kind of fast," because at that point, the conversation—which actually hadn't even started—lapsed. When we finished our brunch, he paid, got up, and said good-bye. It must have been the quickest date on any record, and it also solidified for me the opinion I'd had all along about Match.com. Please take me off of it.

It had never occurred to me that I would ever have sex again as long as I lived. It was astounding enough for me to have found romantic love again when I was older, as I had with Franco, so what else could I possibly want? I put the idea out of my mind permanently, along with any more trips to Internet dating sites.

And then I signed up to take courses at the Adult Education Center.

Dear Franco,

A few months ago, I started taking classes at the Adult Education Center, a place I like to call the Old People's School, since pretty much everybody here has gray hair. One of my courses this semester is Dante, and I am using your book from high school in Rome. All the pages are yellow and crackly, and your handwritten notes are all over the place. We're reading the *Inferno* in English, of course, but I like referring to your notes in the margins of the original poem in Italian.

I am also taking a course on the poetry of Yeats, and there is someone in that class whom I've gotten to know and gotten to like. You have been gone a while now, and I think you would not be unhappy that I have found someone else I care about. Remember how many months—really, how many years—that you were not doing well and we could hardly ever go out?

Remember how we had subscription tickets to the concerts at Symphony Hall, and then you decided you didn't want to go anymore? You started to complain that someone with strong garlic breath was always seated close to you, and that made you crazy, given your firmly held opinions about the use or, as you'd say, overuse of garlic in this country. You wanted to stay home, sit in an easy chair, and listen to the same music on a CD. The garlic smell was an easy excuse to stop our subscription, but we both knew it was really because you were feeling too weak to go out. I continued going to the concerts by myself for another season, then stopped to stay home and listen to CDs with you. I have to admit, though, I missed my trips to Symphony Hall a lot, Franco, because you know how much I love classical music. And even though I enjoyed listening to CDs with you, there is just something about being in that gorgeous place, not only to hear the music swelling around the walls, but also to gaze up at those wonderful statues surrounding the balcony. All this is to say that I started again, just this fall, to get season tickets with my new companion. He is as avid a music lover as I am. And our seats are just one row from where you and I used to sit, years ago. I know you would understand.

Then, remember when you needed long periods of rest, and it became impossible for us to go to a play or a movie or a restaurant? Well, that has changed for me now, too, because I have found someone who likes to do all those things. We have seen some plays and a lot of movies together and, believe it or not, go out to eat pretty often. I've discovered so many new restaurants I didn't know existed. That is really due to him and his love of cooking and good food. He is an excellent cook and has made a lot of great meals for me. And guess what? In his kitchen, among his many cookbooks, I found two of yours.

I jokingly call him my "boyfriend," and for him, I am the "girlfriend." It reminds me of that essay I wrote not long after I met you, the one where I pondered what names older men and women, like us, would use to introduce their new love to their friends and acquaintances. All kinds of ideas popped up, like *swain* and *beau* and *consort* and many more. You liked calling yourself "the insignificant other," but of course I would never have allowed that. We were so lucky to find each other; those years together were such an unexpected gift for both of us.

It is hard for me to believe that it is happening all over again, Franco, but I don't think you would disapprove.

CPSIA information can be obtained at www.ICGtesting.com
Printed in the USA
BVOW02s2355190416

444875BV00001B/3/P